THE FAITHS
VARIETIES OF CHRISTIAN EXPRESSION

Edited by L. P. JACKS
M.A., LL.D.

THE PRESBYTERIAN CHURCHES

THE
PRESBYTERIAN
CHURCHES

BY

JAMES MOFFATT

D.D., D.Litt.

WASHBURN PROFESSOR OF CHURCH HISTORY,
UNION THEOLOGICAL SEMINARY, NEW YORK

SECOND EDITION

METHUEN & CO. LTD.
36 ESSEX STREET W.C.
LONDON

First Published . . February 9th 1928
Second Edition . .   1928

" He sent and called the presbyters of the church. And when they were come to him, he said unto them,

" Take heed unto yourselves, and to all the flock, over the which the Holy Spirit hath made you bishops, to feed the church of God, which he hath purchased with his own blood. . . .

" Of your own selves shall men arise speaking perverse things, to draw away disciples after them. Therefore watch. . . .

" And now, brethren, I commend you to God, and to the word of his grace, which is able to build you up, and to give you an inheritance among all them which are sanctified."

St. Paul in *The Acts of the Apostles* (xx. 17–32).

" The presbyters which are among you I exhort, who am also a presbyter, and a witness of the sufferings of Christ, and also a partaker of the glory that shall be revealed :

" Feed the flock of God which is among you, taking the oversight thereof, not by constraint, but willingly ; not for filthy lucre, but of a ready mind ; neither as being lords over God's heritage, but being ensamples to the flock. And when the chief Shepherd shall appear, ye shall receive a crown of glory that fadeth not away."

St. Peter in *The First Epistle of St. Peter* (v. 1–4).

" Obedience ought to be rendered to those presbyters who are within the Church, who have their succession from the apostles, and who, with their episcopal succession, have received the sure spiritual gift of the truth, according to the good pleasure of the Father ; as for the rest, who abandon the original succession and gather in any place whatsoever, they are to be suspected, either as heretics of wrong opinions, or as separatists, proud persons who please themselves, or as hypocrites, acting in this way for the sake of gain or vainglory. From all such we must withdraw, adhering to those who guard the teaching of the apostles, and who, with their presbyterian order, manifest sound speech and a blameless life. . . . Where one may find such, Paul teaches in these words : *God hath set in his church first apostles, then prophets, thirdly teachers*. So where the spiritual gifts of the Lord have been set, there ought we to learn the truth, in the company of those who have the church-succession from the apostles, who maintain sound and irreproachable behaviour, and with whom pure and incorruptible discourse is known to abide. For such men guard our faith in the one God who made all things, and increase our devotion to the Son of God who hath wrought so greatly for us, and expound to us the scriptures without blaspheming God or dishonouring the patriarchs or despising the prophets."

St. Irenæus : *Adversus Omnes Hæreses*, iv. 26.

EDITOR'S PREFACE

A WORD of explanation seems to be needed in regard to the title and the sub-title which have been chosen for this series.

There is *one* faith, says St. Paul ; but the title of the series indicates more than one. A difficulty unquestionably exists at that point. It has not been overlooked.

Had the promoters of this series adopted the former point of view and called it ' the Faith ' instead of ' the Faiths ', they would have answered in advance an important question which the series itself should be left to answer. But, equally, by calling the series ' the Faiths ', instead of ' the Faith ', have they not prejudged the question in another way ?

Of the two positions the latter seemed the less dogmatic. Let us take the world as we find it, in which the Faiths show themselves as a plurality, and then, if they are really one, or many varieties of the same, or if only one is true and the rest false, let the fact appear from the accounts they give of themselves.

On no other terms could full liberty have been accorded to the writers who contribute to the series ; on no other terms could the task of editing the series be fairly carried out.   It would have been obviously unfair to demand of each of the contributors that he should exhibit the faith that is in him as ultimately identical with the faith that is in each of his fellow-contributors.   It would have been obviously unfair to deny to any contributor the right to exhibit his own faith as the only true faith and all the rest as false.   It would have been obviously unfair to assume that faith is necessarily singular because St. Paul so describes it.   For the degree of authority to be attributed to the words of St. Paul is precisely one of the points on which the contributors to the series must be allowed to differ and to speak for themselves.

The same considerations apply to the sub-title of the series—' Varieties of Christian Expression '. It may be that Christianity has only *one* mode of expression, and that it ceases to be Christianity when expressed in any other way.   But to take that for granted would ill become the editor of such a series as this, and it would become him still worse if he deliberately planned the series so as to lead up to that conclusion.   Again we must take the world as we find it.   Among those who claim to be Christians many varieties of expression unquestionably exist which may or may not be only different ways of expressing the same original truth.   So far as the editor is concerned this must be left an open question.   If to some writers in the series it should seem good to deny the name of Christian to those whose modes of expression differ from their own, they must not be precluded from doing so, and the reader will judge for himself between the claim and the counter-claim. Certainly the hope is entertained that from the presentation of differences in this series there may emerge some unities hitherto unsuspected or dimly seen ; but that will be as it may. The issue is not to be forced.

To present a complete logical justification of our title and sub-title is perhaps not possible, and such justification as we have here offered will probably commend itself only to the pragmatic mind. But objections taken to these titles will be found on examination to be objections to the series itself. How, we might ask, can any earnest and eminent Christian, believing his own variety of Christian expression to be better than the rest, logically justify his co-operation, in such a series as this, with other earnest and eminent Christians whose beliefs in that matter run counter to his own ? None the less they are here co-operating.

That such co-operation has been found possible may be reckoned one of the signs of the times. The explanation of it lies, not in logic, but in charity.

L. P. JACKS

CONTENTS

The Presbyterian Churches

CHAPTER I

INTRODUCTION

PRESBYTERIANISM is the name for belief in the apostolic and catholic Church as governed by presbyters. There may be higher offices in the Church, occupied by individual presbyters for a time or even permanently, but there is no higher order of the Christian ministry than that of presbyters, who discharge the full functions of that ministry, administering the sacraments, preaching the Word, ordaining to the ministry, caring for the souls of their people, supervising the discipline, service, and enterprise of the Church. Such is the characteristic note of Presbyterian polity. The Presbyterian Churches are not invariably called Presbyterian, but Presbyterian churchmen agree that the full functions and responsibilities of the apostolic ministry belong to presbyters as such.

These Presbyterian Churches, in which millions from many tongues and nations are united to Christ, are ' particular Churches ' (as they used to say in the sixteenth and seventeenth centuries), that is, branches of the one Church which, as we look at the apostolic age, we feel bound to recognize as ' Presbyterian '. It is the business of this book to define somehow the sense and reason of this interpretation. And obviously, at the outset, what differentiates the Presbyterian Churches from others is not a matter of creed but of constitution. Like every living organization they have developed practical forms of vitality and self-expression, distinctive of their polity. These constitutive principles, as they are now in operation, may be described as follows : (a) the parity of presbyters ; (b) the right of the people, through their representatives or lay elders, to take part in the government of the Church ; and (c) the unity of the Church, not simply in faith and order, but in a graduated series of Church courts which express and exercise the common authority of the Church as a divine society. 'We hold to a *jure divino* form of Church government, so far as these principles go ',[1] said Dr. Charles Hodge in last century, the able American exponent of the Presbyterian faith. To-day most Presbyterians would probably fight shy of the ' *jus divinum* ' phrase in this connexion ; it witnesses to a truth, as the ' divine right of kings ' once did in politics, but it has become so liable to misconception that they prefer to avoid it and to say, with the Book of Church Order of the Presbyterian Church in the United States (1879), that while ' the Church which the Lord Jesus Christ has erected in this world for the gathering and perfecting of the saints is His visible kingdom of grace ', the ' scriptural doctrine of Presbytery is necessary to the perfection of the order of the visible Church, but is not essential to its existence '. However, this threefold summary of fundamental features holds good for all Presbyterian Churches as they live and move. It is brief. But then, as Francis Rous, the Provost of Eton, observed in one of his

[1] *The Church and its Polity*, p. 125.

books—and Rous was for a time a right zealous Presbyterian—'a little boat may land men on a large continent'. The worth and working of the Presbyterian Churches is indeed a large continent, and this summary will land readers on it as comfortably and effectively as any other.

Naturally the ethos of the Presbyterian Churches varies to some extent. Each has its cherished associations and idiosyncrasies, according to the past history of its country and the traditions of its origin. How different, for example, are the setting and attitude of the Swiss Churches and those on the American continent! And how apart is the Presbyterian Church in England from either! Yet there is a common denominator for these and for all the Churches in the Presbyterian communion. If I illustrate my point here and there from the Scottish Churches in particular, it is because I have been born and trained there, not because my loyalty has narrowed my appreciation of other branches. I wish to make that clear at the very start. Naturally one can speak best of the Church traditions which one knows from the inside.

'Church traditions' I say deliberately. For the Presbyterian Churches are Churches. That is one clue to the common ethos of their gains and pains, as they have survived and thriven in history. Where they are forced, or where they allow themselves to slip, into the position of a mere sect—I do not mean in the sense of a religious minority or of one Church among others, but in the sense of a sectarian outlook upon national and missionary responsibilities—they inevitably decline. Their numbers may keep up, as a religious club keeps up, and they may have a name to live. But in parting with the consciousness of a catholic Church, which has duties to all classes and conditions in the land, they part with what is vital to their identity. Calvinists and Lutherans amid all their differences have been agreed, from the outset, that the Church is not a mere conventicle, a self-started body of ' pious variers from the Church ', gathered round some ' heated pulpiteer ', or of provincial religionists who belong to one class in the main. The spirit of the authentic creeds, confessions, and testimonies of the Presbyterian Churches may be summed up in the words of the apostle, ' I speak of Christ and of the Church '. The witness to Christ is primary ; it is the evangelical, spiritual apprehension of what Christ is and does, of His saving presence and authority in the Word and the sacraments, that Presbyterian churchmen seek to conserve. But in their preaching and teaching they also speak of ' the Church ', of Christ in the first place, but not without the Church of which He is Head and Lord, and through which as His Body He works for men. One of our own Swiss theologians, the brilliant Alexandre Vinet, expressed this fundamental belief as follows : ' It is the Church that saves you, because it is she who brings you Jesus Christ. We rejoice to maintain that the relations of the believer with the Living Water, which is Christ, are immediate, but the Church, that is to say the Christian community, in the succession of the centuries, is the torrent or stream which brings down to you the name and the knowledge of Jesus Christ, and, so to speak, Jesus Christ Himself. Without the Church no Christianity and no Christians ! '

In a series like the present it is inevitable that one has to define Presbyterianism now and then by mentioning that it is not this or that. As the schoolmen used to explain, all definition is negation. But negation in this case is not equivalent to defiance and disparagement. It is worse than idle to recommend any constructive polity of the Great House by presenting it so that it resembles the palace in *Rasselas*, 'built as if Suspicion herself had dictated the plan '. Part of this book has had to be devoted to a comparison and contrast between the Presbyterian Churches in history and their rivals. But historical facts were never meant to be used as stones of offence by any one Church ; they are stepping-stones. Those which I have chosen here will show how as Presbyterian churchmen we have picked our way and propose to pick it still. We think they are laid in an authentic line from the apostolic faith of the Church. If this means that now and then we are not prepared to step out exactly as some of our fellow-Christians are doing, it does not imply that we question the legitimacy or doubt the efficacy of their convictions, even although we feel ourselves bound to believe that ours is in some essential respects a truer testimony to the original constitution of the Church. A contributor to this series does best by stating unambiguously the characteristics of his own ecclesiastical position and the principles which differentiate it from other communions. As a Presbyterian churchman I have tried to explain where we stand, explicitly and definitely, but, I trust, without any tinge of acerbity. We seek to commend our heritage, and this ought to be compatible with true catholicity of spirit. To be spineless is one extreme, to be spiky is another, in matters ecclesiastical.

I have no claim whatever to write officially for

B

Presbyterianism.   Neither am I expected to provide an historical conspectus, such as Dr. J. N. Ogilvie has done so competently in *The Presbyterian Churches of Christendom*.   This book is no more than a short study of the faith and worship and service of our Churches. I hope it may remove some of the odd misconceptions which are still lingering in certain quarters, for such misconceptions are the soil of prejudice and misunderstanding.   But I also hope that this exposition of the Church principles for which and by which we stand may be of service to some within our own gates.   While a Church like the Presbyterian Church is tempted by its self-consciousness to exaggerate and stiffen the statement of its characteristics in controversy, it may be prone to whittle them away in the opposite mood of warm sympathy with the spirit and aims of some Christian organizations in its neighbourhood.   Now, nothing is gained by showing a sectional or insular temper in any discussion of the Christian Church.   But a Church is a Church, not an amorphous association floating on the tides of undenominationalism.   Nor is it a collection of pious particles.   I have heard of a Highland minister who in his prayer of intercession besought the Lord's mercy upon men suffering from various ills, and finally interceded on behalf of those who were 'mere individuals'.   If the Presbyterian Church is to remain true to its principles of the Church as part of its witness to the Gospel, it must on no account crumble into pious individualism any more than it dare stiffen itself into a clerical corporation. In these latter days the former is a subtle temptation. So I have sometimes written with an eye to those whose generous appreciation of any form of contemporary Christian work is more conspicuous than their grasp of what our great forefathers meant the Church to be, as well as to some who are none the worse of being reminded—if I may cite our own Vinet once again—that when they begin to take an interest in their Church they will be nearer than is commonly supposed to feeling an interest in religion.

CHAPTER II

IN THE BEGINNING

WHAT a modern student would call orders or constituted offices ranked less, in the apostolic Churches, than special gifts, e.g. of prophecy. These were conspicuous and effective endowments, which in course of time passed away or changed their form. Much was provisional, as indeed could not but be the case, when the eschatological hope still flamed high. In the Epistles there are several references to the various kinds of Christian work in which members were expected to take part, according to their qualifications, but the terms employed are generally fluid and unofficial. So long as the primitive apostles were alive, planting Christianity in various fields, and organizing their converts, the position resembled that of a modern foreign mission, where the missionaries evangelize the natives, till a native Church arises with its self-government. As we put aside the branches and look down into the pool of the primitive Church, we see the apostles divinely commissioned for the Church at large, doing the work of evangelists, founding Churches by the authority of the Lord. The ministers of these Churches appear to have been appointed and at first supervised, or rather reinforced, by them. Then the further stage comes when the initial phase passes, and the Churches develop, with ministers who possess all that is transmissible or permanently needful for the Church in the apostolic office. These ministers or presbyters are in the apostolic succession, as they exercise their full ministerial functions of service and leadership in the ministry of the Word and the sacraments. The primitive apostolic office had elements which were special to itself; no one could succeed to the privilege of having seen the Lord, for example. But all that was transmissible in their ministry passed to those who were called to serve in their Churches, and part of this ministerial function was to pass it on duly, i.e. in a regular and responsible way. Those who had been commissioned by the apostles to the ministry, commissioned others in turn 'for the perfecting of the saints, for the work of the ministry, for the edifying of the Body of Christ'. It is natural to infer this from the available data, and there is nothing to contradict it in the contemporary evidence.

The primitive ministry of the Church was no problem to its own age, but it has been a vexed problem to later generations. It would be irrelevant to linger in this debatable, intricate land of controversy over the early Christian ministry. All we can do is to give a concise epitome, as dispassionate as possible, in the light of modern research which has so notably confirmed the Presbyterian interpretation at some salient points.

The first Church history is the so-called Acts of the Apostles. We open it, to find that when the Church of Antioch subscribed to the fund in relief of their starving fellow-Christians in Judæa, they sent their contribution 'to the presbyters' of the Church at Jerusalem. Who they were, and how they had come

into existence, the historian does not explain. Possibly
they were the gifted 'seven' (so-called deacons) who
had already been appointed at Jerusalem to superintend
the funds and food of the local community. At any
rate, they share with the apostles in the authority of
the Church; thus it is 'the apostles and the presbyters
as fellow-Christians' (this is the force of the term
'brethren' after these words) who issue the authoritative
decree of the first Council of Jerusalem. The apostles
do not act here by themselves. Presbyters were also
in charge of Churches outside Jerusalem; they were
not a local peculiarity. In one of his rare allusions to
Church government among the Pauline Churches, the
historian mentions that on their return visit to Lystra,
Iconium, and Antioch, Paul and Barnabas chose presbyters for the local Christians in every Church. This
must have been the normal practice. Wherever we
look in the Epistles, the Church is ruled by presbyters,
in Asia (1 Peter v. 1–3), for example, and in the Churches
to which the pastoral homily or Epistle of James is
directed. Whether John the presbyter, who wrote the
2nd and 3rd Epistles of John, was the apostle or not,
his authority over the Churches (presumably those
round Ephesus) is that of a presbyter, as was that of
Peter.

'Presbyters' was a familiar title for officials in the
civic life of the day, among Greeks and Romans; it
was by no means confined to the Jewish synagogue
polity. But, whatever suggested it to the primitive
Church, it rapidly became the name for the responsible
ministers. Originally, like 'aldermen', it connoted age
or seniority, and this association often clung to it, even
when it had become a more or less official title in the

Church. The ' presbyters ' were in the first instance usually chosen from the most experienced members of the community, but the data warrant us in concluding that these presbyters are not simply the senior members of the community, who enjoy deference on account of length of years. The warnings addressed to them and the specific duties expected from them imply that the term ' presbyter ' denotes a class of responsible Church officials. The term ' bishop ' denotes, as the Greek (*episcopos*, overseer, president) implies, the character of their office, which was to supervise the community; theirs was a cure of souls, a pastoral ministry. The presbyter might be termed, in the primitive days, either ' bishop ' or ' ruler ' or ' shepherd ', for none of these terms marked a separate and special office, but merely functions of the presbyteral ministry. When the term ' overseer ' or ' bishop ' was used (or the verb allied to that noun), it referred invariably to the oversight of God's people by presbyters, not to any oversight exercised over presbyters themselves.

In the Pastoral Epistles, which are more explicit on questions of Church order than any other documents of the period, there are two orders of ministry, presbyters (or bishops) and deacons; the main distinction between them is that the deacons do not teach. The duty of Christian instruction is confined to the presbyters; ability to teach and to argue, or to impart Christian truth, is a primary requisite for the presbyter as an overseer or ' bishop '. Little else is said about their functions; good moral character, capacity, and the teaching gift are to the front in the list of qualifications.

The last-named is particularly prominent. In the

history of the Presbyterian Churches it has been steadily
recognized, so that their preaching, which includes what
the primitive Church knew as prophetic and as teaching
ministries, has been upon an unusually high level.   This
stress on instruction emerges repeatedly in the Pastoral
Epistles. ' Let the elders that rule well be counted
worthy of double honour, especially they who labour
in the word and doctrine.' This text, which was
greatly over-worked in the earlier stages of the Presbyterian controversy, does not distinguish two classes of
elders, ruling and teaching ; as the context shows, it
pleads for ample remuneration (this is the sense of
' double honour ') being given to presbyters who are
efficient presidents or superintendents, ' particularly to
those who have the task of preaching and teaching ' ;
apparently some presbyters had not the same gift of
popular instruction as others, or were content to devolve
the latter duty on some of their fellows.   It is one
interest of these Epistles to make presbyters conscious
of their responsibility for teaching.   The presbyter as
overseer or ' bishop ' must be ' apt to teach '.   Presiding
over the worship and discipline of the Church was one
of their important duties, but evidently the need was
felt for such officers of the Church controlling the
instruction, in view of dangers arising from loose teaching by vagrant evangelists and lecturers on religion.
The fact that the presbyters are to be supported by the
congregations whom they thus inspire and instruct is,
by the way, an incidental proof that they were regarded
as apostolic ministers, for it was apostles in the primitive
Churches who possessed this right.

The Pastoral Epistles are late documents of the period,
in their present form ; still, as one of the most recent

Roman Catholic scholars, Professor Emil Metzner, observes, in his acute critique of Harnack, ' presbyter ' and ' bishop ' are not yet anything but terms for the same official of the Church. ' All Catholic theologians understand *episcopus* in the Epistle to Timotheus and Titus in the later sense of the term [i.e. in the monarchical]. This view is also defended in textbooks of dogma. . . . But it is obviously an error ; neither Titus nor Timotheus appointed bishops, in the later sense of the term, during Paul's lifetime, but only presbyters '.[1]

The only critical question is, whether the Pastoral Epistles do not represent Timotheus or Titus as possessed of special powers, which place them in a direct apostolic succession, to which presbyters owe their position but to which they cannot attain. What we seem to see is that Titus is commissioned for a time to appoint presbyters in every town of Crete, and Timotheus is warned against ' laying hands suddenly ' on anyone ; the latter phrase may mean the ordination of presbyters. Obviously their functions, as contemplated in these documents, were quasi-apostolic ; they selected, ordained, and superintended the local presbyters, as well as exercising supervision generally over the Churches. But it was not so much an institution as a measure of administration, to meet some passing emergency. Timotheus had been ordained by a presbytery, with the laying-on of hands, and at this service Paul had been present, for he speaks, or is made to speak, of ' the divine gift (or charism) which you received when my hands were laid upon you '. This gift he is to re-kindle. But it is the gift of grace which qualifies

[1] *Die Verfassung der Kirche in den zwei ersten Jahrhunderten* (1920), p. 42.

for a consecrated ministry, not any specific commission to ordain. He and Titus are to do for these districts what Paul had done elsewhere. The work thus assigned to them was a temporary duty ; the former was to rejoin St. Paul, and the latter was not permanently resident in Crete. Their quasi-apostolic responsibilities at Ephesus and in Crete were an emergency measure, which invested them with special powers, for the time being, such as a rapidly developing mission may require in certain fields. 'The more I study these Pastoral Epistles', says Dr. T. M. Lindsay,[1] ' the more evident it becomes to me that they are just what every experienced missionary has to impart to a younger and less experienced colleague when he warns him about the difficulties that he must face and the tasks, often unexpected, he will find confronting him. It is scarcely to be wondered at then that the Pastoral Epistles are always among the earliest portions of the Scriptures translated in almost every Christian mission.'

This view of their functions is borne out by a document which lies on the border of the apostolic age. Some time before the end of the first century, in all likelihood, the Church of Corinth deposed some of its presbyters. The Church of Rome, through a certain Clement, addressed a friendly remonstrance against this action on the part of what it considered ' a few audacious upstarts ' ; it does not protest against the action itself, as though the Church had exceeded its power, but against a hasty, unfair exercise of power by these conceited juniors. The epistle throws light upon the constitution of the Corinthian Church. Its ruling authorities are presbyters, whose office of oversight is termed *episcopê*. Upstart persons are bidden, ' submit yourselves to the presbyters ' (57) ; ' let the flock of

---

[1] *The Church and the Ministry in the Early Centuries*, p. 141.

Christ be at peace with the presbyters set over it' (54).
Once only does Clement call them *episcopoi* (42), and
there because he is interested in citing a far-fetched and
illusory prophecy of the title from the Greek version of
Isaiah lx. 17; the presbyters are *episcopoi* or 'bishops'
to him exactly as the presbyters of the Ephesian Church
were to St. Paul, charged with spiritual oversight.   There
is not a syllable about any monarchical or diocesan bishop.

According to Clement (42) the first presbyters were
appointed by the apostles, who were duly preaching the
Gospel ; ' they went out with complete assurance of the
Holy Spirit to preach the Gospel' (*N.B.*, nothing is said of
any special sacramental function or interest), ' and as
they preached through country districts and towns they
would appoint their first converts, after testing them by
the Spirit, to be bishops and deacons of those who were to
believe'.   They then (43), he adds, took the further
precaution, in order to prevent strife and disorder, of
enacting that ' if they (i.e. these original presbyters)
died, other tested persons should succeed to their ministry'.
This proves that the apostolic succession is simply the
succession of presbyters to presbyters, the first of whom
had been appointed by the apostles.   Nothing is said
about any transmission of powers.   Clement's conclusion
is simply that it is wrong to remove from the ministry
' those whom they (i.e. the apostles) appointed, or who
were afterwards appointed by other notable men, with
the consent of the whole Church, persons who have served
the flock of God blamelessly, humbly, quietly, and without
presumption '.   Apparently the deposed presbyters at
Corinth were partly men appointed by the apostles and
partly by their successors.   But who were these successors
or ' notable men ' to whom Clement refers so vaguely ?
Coadjutors of the apostles, like Timotheus and Titus
(according to one view of the Pastoral Epistles), who were
specially delegated to transmit some apostolic commission,
a body of men set up with quasi-apostolic powers to make
ministerial appointments ?   Or, influential members of the
congregation, perhaps local prophets and teachers, an

elective board of trustworthy Christians who filled up the vacancies as they occurred ? Or, as has been assumed above, the presbyters themselves who had been appointed by the apostles ? The first theory, and possibly the second, would require the words 'if they died' to refer to the apostles themselves, which is next to impossible. The second theory, that these persons were not necessarily appointed by the apostles, but represented the more influential members of the local Church, who filled up vacancies as they arose, with the consent and concurrence of the congregation, has much more in its favour than the narrower hypothesis of special apostolic commissioners, which would only be tenable were there any reference to them elsewhere. Now, as it happens, Clement does allude twice to 'rulers' of the Church in connexion with presbyters : 'you lived by the laws of God, obeying your rulers and paying due honour to your presbyters', (1) and 'let us respect the rulers, let us honour the presbyters' (21). In both cases the allusion is followed up by a reference to 'the younger men', or juniors, who are to be disciplined into respect. This proves that 'presbyter' is used not only as an official title, but with a special stress also on its original connotation of 'senior'; as was apt, for the arbitrary action in the Corinthian Church had been the work of younger men. But 'rulers' is probably a generic term for presbyters, prophets, teachers, and other specially influential men in the community. There is no foundation, so far as I see, for the hypothesis that it refers to any special body like the 'notable men', taken as delegates with quasi-apostolic authority, for Clement never once appeals to such a body, and one can hardly be asked seriously to believe that this failure on his part was due to the fact that none of them chanced to be in Corinth at the moment ! He does not appeal to them to exercise their authority, for the simple reason that they did not exist.

The choice appears to lie between the second and the third of these interpretations. Either fits in with that dispassionate view of the primitive ministry which is all that Presbyterianism requires. Such a view leaves much uncertain, as indeed any view must, which would avoid anachronisms. But two negative conclusions emerge. One is (i) that there is no evidence of any apostle having ever set aside any official in the early Church to administer the Eucharist. However, the worship of the Church came eventually to be dominated by the Eucharist, and thereby to affect the conception of the ministry, it is significant that the records of the apostolic Church offer no support to the theory that the administration of the Sacrament was devolved by the apostles as a special function upon any group of ministers. The local ministry must have baptized. Otherwise how could any converts have been baptized at all in the Pauline Churches, when the apostle himself very rarely baptized? And, as in these primitive days the baptism of adults was at once followed by participation in the Eucharist, the admission of catechumens by any rite of confirmation would inevitably fall to the presbyters. These conclusions may seem inferences and assumptions, but they are such inferences as an historian of institutions is justified in drawing from the scanty data at his command, and they are already assumed by the writers of the primitive records, who are silent upon such procedure simply because they did not require to chronicle it.

The other (ii) conclusion from an examination of the extant historical data is, that no satisfactory evidence is forthcoming for the hypothesis that as the apostolate expired its general functions were transmitted to a body corresponding to the later episcopate. Neither the Pastoral Epistles nor the Epistle of Clement yield any decisive evidence that the apostles transmitted to bishops through any group of ' apostolic men ' a special endowment of ordination for presbyters and other Church officers in general. As the apostles fade from the scene, the presbyters remain and continue. ' We need not hesitate to regard them as having been from the first ministers of the sacraments ', Dr. Gore admits.[1] If so, we need not hesitate to conclude, with Clement of Rome, that they could and did ordain.

For reasons into which it is not needful here to enter, the Church of the second century began to develop what is variously called monarchical or diocesan episcopacy, or monepiscopacy, i.e. a single ' bishop ' ruling the Church, with a college or presbytery of presbyters under him. It is disputed whether this ' bishop ' was one of the presbyters raised to the rank of perpetual president, or the successor of the apostles directly, through some body of ' apostolic commissioners '. In any case, the development of this episcopacy was gradual and limited. Thus the Church of Philippi, down into the second century, continued to be served by presbyters and deacons, as we see from a letter to it written by Polycarp, the Bishop of Smyrna. There was no monarchical or diocesan Bishop at Philippi ; the Church was superintended by presbyters. St. Paul, nearly a century earlier, had called them ' bishops ' (Philippians i. 1), but Polycarp avoids giving them this title, since ' bishop ' was now becoming the name for a separate, special position such as he himself held at Smyrna. Yet he never suggests that the Church of Philippi was not a Church, because it had no bishop. Logically, Ignatius would have had to do so. But his

[1] *The Church and the Ministry* (1919), p. 239.

sweeping statement about bishops being 'appointed throughout the world' (*Eph.* 3) is pious rhetoric; it shows how little he knew about the real constitution of Churches outside Syria and Asia Minor. Probably he was referring simply to communities with which he was familiar, and in which the monarchical episcopate had been set up. The good man must have had his eyes opened when he reached Philippi on his way to martyrdom at Rome, although history does not record whether or not he modified his earlier assertion that there could be no Church apart from 'bishop, presbyters, and deacons' (*Trall.*, 3).

It seems to be the same with the Church of Rome, as we see it in *The Shepherd* of Hermas, an important second-century Church document. Renan actually thought that Hermas, who was himself a presbyter, was opposed to the monarchical episcopate on principle : 'il semble avoir été de ceux qui firent opposition à l'institution naissante qui renversait l'égalité des "presbyters"' (*L'Église Chrétienne*, p. 420). However this may be, he represents the Church as ruled by presbyters alone (in *Vis.* ii. 4. 3). At Alexandria the presbyters appear to have long exercised some of their ancient privileges, although the surviving evidence for this is curious and conflicting.

However, it is superfluous to enter into any further details. The object of this rapid summary or outline is simply to indicate how the data of the Church are patient of a Presbyterian interpretation, in the days when it was under the sway of the first apostles. This interpretation is not a mere reading back of modern preconceptions into ancient documents. 'It is most manifestly proved', says Jerome, writing as an exegete of the New Testament, ' that bishop and presbyter are the same '. Custom had assigned the bishop some special prerogatives, by the fourth century, within the order of presbyters to which he belonged, but Jerome knew that it had not been always so ; in the apostolic Church presbyters were bishops, the only bishops known to the Church at large.   In the New Testament, Dr. Hort sums up, ' we find nothing that points to an institution or system ' higher than that of the presbyters, ' nothing like the episcopal system of later times '.[1]   ' In the language of the New Testament ', said Bishop Lightfoot, commenting on Philippians i. 1, ' the same officer in the Church is called indifferently " bishop " and " elder " or " presbyter " '.   ' The particular point to emphasize ', as the Bishop of Gloucester puts it in his Bampton Lectures, ' is that the original and official name was " presbyter ", and that other titles, such as " episcopos " and " pastor ", were used as descriptive designations '.[2]

[1] *The Christian Ecclesia*, p. 232.
[2] *The Doctrine of the Church and Reunion*, p. 66.

CHAPTER III

ON THE CONTINENT

IN his essay on Private Judgment, Newman asked his readers to understand by the 'Church' what Scripture meant. 'We hear much of Bible Christians, Bible religion, Bible preaching; it would be well if we heard a little of the Bible Church also.' What Newman asked, in 1841, was the very thing which the Reformers had been forward to do in the sixteenth century. They opened their Bibles, and found little or nothing there corresponding to the ecclesiastical system which had been constructed during the Middle Ages; they also caught glimpses of a Bible Church which had been dimmed and even distorted. I have already, in the Introduction, mentioned the three conceptions of the Church's powers and polity which are innate in Presbyterianism. These three principles became blunted or obliterated during the course of the Middle Ages in Europe, until the Western Church had to be re-formed in order to recover them. It is not for us here to trace the process, but merely to indicate its general trend.

(*a*) The apostolic function of the presbyters had been restricted by the devolution of certain rights and duties upon the bishop. Jurisdiction was one. 'Every student of the Canon Law knew the doctrine that the prelacy of bishops is founded, not on divine command,

C

but on " a custom of the Church " '.[1]   Yet more than jurisdiction was at stake ; or, to put it more accurately, jurisdiction involved some serious consequences for the Christian ministry.

It was the great Swiss Presbyterian scholar, F. Godet, of Neuchâtel, who recognized that the parable in St. Luke xii. 41–48 implied a ministry in succession to the apostles.   The words involve, he remarks in his *Commentary on St. Luke's Gospel* (English translation, vol. ii, p. 108), ' that the apostolate will be perpetuated till the return of Christ ; and the figure employed does indisputably prove that there will subsist in the Church to the very end a ministry of the Word established by Christ.   Of this the apostles were so well aware that when they were themselves leaving the earth they took care to establish ministers of the Word to fill their places in the Church.   This ministry was a continuation, if not of their whole office, at least of one of its most indispensable functions, that of which Jesus speaks in this parable—the regular distribution of spiritual nourishment to the flock.   The theory which makes the ministry emanate from the Church as its representative is therefore not Biblical ; the office is rather an emanation from the apostolate, and thus mediately an institution of Jesus Himself '.   This was sound Presbyterian doctrine, as old as George Gillespie, the Scottish churchman of the seventeenth century, who in 1642 quoted St. Luke xii. 42 (' Who then is that faithful and wise steward, whom his Lord shall make ruler over his household, to give them their portion of meat in due season ? ') to prove that more than gifts and abilities were required for the Christian ministry.

[1] F. W. Maitland, *The Cambridge Modern History*, ii. 594.

'Stewards' were to be appointed by the Lord for the
purpose of dispensing food to the rest of the members
of God's household; 'it is not Christ's will that anyone
of the household who is faithful, wise, and discreet,
may take upon himself the steward's office; there is a
steward constituted and appointed for the purpose', as
there shall be to the end. And, Gillespie adds, 'there
is nothing which more properly belongeth to the
ecclesiastical stewards than the dispensation of the
sacraments'.[1]

This interpretation of the parable, which makes the
Christian ministry, in Godet's words, 'une émanation
de l'apostolat', is more than modern historical scholarship would probably allow. What the language of the
parable implies is that the apostles will be responsible
for the Church, and either that they will live to see the
Lord's return or that there will be such faithful stewards
always in the community; any such minister, whether
chosen by the Church or not, is appointed by the Lord.
This seems all that is fairly covered by the parable
itself. But I quote the interpretation to show how
deep and serious a view Presbyterian churchmen took
of the ministry as apostolic, and how instinctively they
resented any limitation of its functions or Church
duties, such as the hierarchical system had involved.
When presbyters were denied the right of commissioning
to the ministry, for example, this was held to be an
infringement of the original apostolic constitution. Yet
even the original right was not without a witness.
'Each bishop ordained his own presbyters, along with
the college of presbyters', Calvin explains (*Inst.*, IV.

[1] In a Treatise printed in *The Presbyterian's Armoury* (1846).

iv. 15). ' But although they all did the same act, yet
as the bishop presided and as the ordination was carried
out, as it were, under his auspices, it was on that account
said to be his.' In ordaining, it was claimed, the
bishop by canonical law had been really acting as a
presbyter among his fellow-presbyters. This is what
Dr. John Duncan meant by saying that ' all Christendom
becomes Presbyterian on an ordination day '.[1] It
becomes semi-Presbyterian, anyhow.

One curious survival of the primitive authority of
presbyters, even after ordination had been restricted
to bishops, may be mentioned. In the Celtic Church
of the West, during its long, brilliant monastic period,
whilst a bishop was retained in each monastery for
purposes of ordination, out of deference to the current
practice of the Church, he had no diocesan duties or
rights ; indeed, he appears to have been no more than
an officer or official under the jurisdiction of the abbot.
It is not accidental, perhaps, that the welcome to the
Reformation proved to be widest in countries which
had been originally evangelized by the monks of the
Irish and Scottish Church.

Presbyterian churchmen would not for a moment
hold that the Church was bereft of the divine guidance,
after the New Testament period ; the institution of
monarchical bishops in the second century may be
amply justified as a measure needful for conserving
discipline, unity, and stability in the chaotic condition
of the age, and the testimony of use and wont for

[1] *Colloquia Peripatetica* (5th edition, 1879), p. 75, a collection
of sayings, edited by Professor William Knight of St. Andrews
University. Dr. Duncan was the first Professor of Hebrew in
the New College, Edinburgh, one of the most erudite linguists
of the day, and a man of quaint, wide philosophic interests.

fifteen centuries in the Western Church is not to be lightly valued. But that this institution is the one safeguard of unity or orthodoxy, and essential to the stability of the Church, is a very different thing. What the Church as a living organization was free to do, in the second and third centuries, it was free to do in the sixteenth, and is still free to do, i.e. to maintain the unity of the faith by reviving what was prior to the monarchical episcopate, in order to carry out as effectively (to put it in the lowest terms) the duty of Christian unity and enterprise. What Presbyterianism maintained from the first was the valid government of the Church, as in the days of the apostles, by presbyters acting conjointly, not by a bishop ruling over presbyters and their congregations.

(b) Then, the conception of the Church became narrowed in many cases to the clergy. The normal meaning of ' the Church ', in the Middle Ages, had been ' the hierarchy '. If you were a churchman, you were an ecclesiastic. Marsilius of Padua, in the *Defensor Pacis*, was one of the first to call attention to this anomaly and error. Few things in his outspoken treatise so startled the fourteenth century as his fresh definition of the Church. Mostly, he confesses, it has come to denote the clergy, presbyters, or bishops (*presbyteros seu episcopos*—for Marsilius generally used *seu* in this collocation, recognizing as a scholar the original implications of these terms), deacons, etc. But, he points out, the primitive and real Church is composed of all faithful followers of Christ, whether clergy or laity ; they are the true ' churchmen ', *viri ecclesiastici.*

The early right of Church members to express their

consent and concurrence, if not to exercise their choice, in the appointment of the clergy, shrank into a mere form, but it persisted, even amid the novelties and alterations of polity which mediæval Europe witnessed within the Western Church. That the appointment of clergy to parishes should pass into the hands of private patrons, for example, was a change which in the later Middle Ages was both questioned and resented by many good churchmen. ' It is quite clear that, to the canonists, the appointment of a Christian minister was really a matter for the Christian people, and that it was to their minds a grave abuse that this appointment should be vested in any single person.' [1] But the abuse prevailed. The laity lost their practical share in electing their ministers. This was owing to their own apathy, it is true, rather than to any aggrandizement on the part of the clergy. Still, the Church failed to sustain in its members that vital, spiritual interest in their Church which produces a sense of responsibility and an active participation in its essential functions. This had to be recovered, by the fresh assertion of the Church as the community of all the faithful, by the restoration to Church members of their rights in the choice of ministers, and of representative self-government by means of elders. In this way the danger of clericalism was averted, so far as it can be averted by any organization of the Church. So long as members of a congregation have the right to elect or nominate not only their deacons and representative elders but their ministers, this direct and prayerful share in the government of the Church renders it ' impossible for the Church courts to degenerate into tyrannical close

[1] Bartlet and Carlyle, *Christianity in History*, p. 367.

corporations, prone to introduce clerical bureaucracy once more into the Church. . . . In Geneva presbytery might be only priest writ large, but in Scotland the constitutional remedy for such a state of ecclesiastical administration lay ever ready in the hands of the Church members themselves '.[1]

(c) Finally, as the people had no lay representatives, the administration of the Church became more and more a matter for the clerical corporation. The jealousy and suspicion of councils in the later Middle Ages proved that the primitive self-government of the Church had been lost sight of. Elaborate systems of corporate action were devised, in terms of the contemporary social and political fabric. But these did not correspond to the self-determination of a living, autonomous Church, such as had been more than an ideal at the beginning. It was this ideal which Presbyterian churchmen at the Reformation set themselves to realize, in terms of their age and situation, by means of Church courts. They did so, from a high view of the Church, not as an ecclesiastical institution, but as the Body of which Christ is the living Head. ' We do not deny ', said Calvin gravely, ' that there are Churches among the papists, even while we are not willing to concede them *simpliciter* the name of Church ' (IV. ii. 12). ' We had to withdraw from them in order to draw near to Christ ', he explains (IV. ii. 6), true to the spirit of the apostolic saying, ' I speak of Christ and of the Church '. And one of the reasons which necessitated this step was the consciousness that the authority of Christ left no place for lordship in His Church.

[1] Dr. Janet G. Macgregor, *The Scottish Presbyterian Polity* (1926), p. 133.

Conciliar government, such as the Presbyterian polity evolved, enabled the Church as a whole to form and express its mind on any subject, under the guidance of its Lord, so that the life and practice of the Church was regulated from within, not from without. The collective expression, arrived at prayerfully and thoughtfully, was to carry authority as it answered to the deepest Christian instincts and interests of the members of the Church.

To sum up. The hierarchical system which had been constructed out of the episcopate was now regarded as invalid ; the Church, as represented by the Reformers, considered the latter to be an innovation and an excrescence, particularly in view of its associations with sacerdotalism. This theory, which Cyprian formulated, was regarded as a further and more serious departure from the original conception of the ministry. Sacerdotalism does not concern us here, except that it rested on a new view of the Eucharist, which evolved into a stiffer centralization and exclusiveness on the part of the Church. Troeltsch [1] is mainly right in tracing the latter to the doctrine of the sacraments. Indeed, the subsequent variations in the theory and practice of the ministry may be best viewed in the light of contemporary sacramental doctrine ; it is the conception of the Sacraments which ultimately determines the mediæval conception of the Christian ministry.

In reconstructing the Church, according to the Word of God, the Reformers, as has been said, were not unmindful of the fact that traces of the original constitution had survived. Thus, between 1384 and 1387

[1] See his *Soziallehren d. Christlichen Kirchen* (p. 88), and his *Die Trennung von Staat und Kirche* (1907).

John de Fordun, a presbyter or chantry priest of the Aberdeen Cathedral, compiled a history of the Scots, *Scotichronicon*, and in this treatise (iii. 8) he reproduced the mediæval view that presbyters were the original order of ministers in the Christian Church. ' In the year of the Lord 430 Pope Celestine sent Saint Palladius into Scotia as the first bishop thereof. . . . Before his arrival the Scots had, as teachers of the faith and administrators of the sacraments, simply presbyters or monks (*presbiteros solummodo vel monachos*), following the rite of the primitive Church (*ritum sequentes ecclesiae primitivae*).' The dominant standard for the Reformers was the Word of God. Historical precedents counted for less. But when they worked out their Church polity, they were not conscious of inventing a novelty ; they were restoring, in terms of the present situation, the original constitution of the holy catholic apostolic Church, reminiscences of which still lingered even within the mediæval fabric, whatever may have been the precise motives which led some mediæval writers to recall this original and apostolic identity of presbyters and bishops.

The continuity of the ministry was assumed. When Calvin speaks of the function of the presbyters, he remarks (*Instit.*, IV. iii. 6) that ' the sacred, inviolable, and lasting law, enjoined upon those who succeed to the place of the apostles (*qui in apostolorum locum succedunt*), is that they receive a commission to preach the Gospel and to administer the sacraments '. Presbyterian churchmen never dreamed of anything else. As ordained ministers they were discharging apostolic functions in the Church, and, as they were not slow to insist, discharging them more adequately than any prelate. It was taken for granted by all that they claimed this position. Indeed, it formed the ground of gibes against them; as when Oliver Cromwell, in lecturing the Little Parliament on July 4, 1653, thanked God that he did not speak 'for a ministry deriving itself from the papacy, and pretending to that which is so much insisted on, "Succession"'. The Protector was referring sarcastically to the Presbyterian ministers of the day. It was a common sneer among the sectaries that the Presbyterians, like the Episcopalians, derived their ministry through the Roman mediæval Church, and Cromwell echoes this, adding, 'The true succession is through the Spirit, given in its measure'—a statement which no Presbyterian would gainsay, since the two are not necessarily incompatible, though when it came to the inspiration of Trusty Tomkins, Master Holdenough might reasonably ask, 'What Spirit'?

No common ground was reached by Presbyterians, however, upon the question of how this apostolic succession was mediated, except that they declined to regard episcopal ordination as essential, thereby anticipating the modern attitude of Anglican High-Churchmen. 'Whereas older Tractarians, like Haddan, made episcopacy an essential part of the succession, the modern High-Churchman is content to regard the succession itself as being the essence, and the exact form of the ministry only secondary'.[1] Indeed, Presbyterians were, as most of them still are, generally content to regard their ministry as valid on the ground that it discharges the essential functions of presbyters as laid down in the Word of God. Since presbytery had a divine right,

[1] Dr. W. H. Frere in *The Church Quarterly Review* (October 1912), pp. 150 f.

it was *ipso facto* valid. Calvin, however, in dismissing
the Roman claim to be the true Church, as being never
destitute of bishops who have followed one another in
an unbroken series, and in declaring that nothing is
more absurd than to disregard doctrine and place
succession in persons, is careful apparently to allow the
possibility that ministerial succession would be valid if
it were accompanied by orthodox doctrine. ' It is vain
to put forward succession unless men retain and remain
in the truth of Christ which they have had handed down
from their fathers, keeping it safe and incorrupted '—as,
he claimed, the re-formed Church did. As a student
of history I doubt if one can fairly interpret the language
of the Scots *Confession* as excluding merely episcopal
succession, although this is maintained by some modern
churchmen.[1] That Confession denies that ' lineal
descent ' is one of the notes of the true Church, and
although in the Latin version this is explained as *successio
episcoporum*, it is doubtful whether the authors did not
mean to deny that any succession was needful to the
being of the true Church. Still, if they did, it was not
a view universally held by Presbyterian churchmen
of that age, or of the succeeding generation. Thus
there is no ambiguity whatever in the Presbyterian
manifesto *Jus Divinum Evangelici Ministerii* or
Regiminis Ecclesiastici (1646). There it is distinctly
claimed that presbyters were in a regular succession
from the apostles ; the argument is stated with the

[1] Statements of this position may be found in Dr. Donald
Macleod's Baird Lectures on *The Doctrine and Validity of the
Ministry and Sacraments of the National Church of Scotland*
(1903), pp. 184 f. ; in Wotherspoon and Kirkpatrick's *Manual
of Church Doctrine*, p. 171 ; and in a recent (1926) pamphlet
on *Presbyterian Orders* (Edinburgh).

patristic and historical learning which Presbyterian churchmen had at their command, and it is further pointed out, just as Calvin had done, that 'the power of ordination exercised for many hundred years by bishops belonged to them as presbyters, not as bishops '.

No mechanical shape or scheme was drawn up for the ministry. According to the Westminster Confession of Faith (i. 6), ' there are some circumstances concerning the worship of God and government of the Church, common to human actions and societies, which are to be ordered by the light of nature and Christian prudence, according to the general rules of the Word, which are always to be observed '. The leading men who organized the Church had too much good sense and scholarship to imagine that it was either possible or desirable to reproduce an exact counterpart of the apostolic Church as it existed in the first century. What the Scottish Reformers in 1558 demanded, for example, was that ' the Church be re-formed in accordance with the precepts of the New Testament, the writings of the Ancient Fathers, and the godly laws of the Emperor Justinian '. Calvin recognized that in the New Testament Churches there were some exceptional precisions and regulations needful for that age ; he was free to allow that in certain cases of ecclesiastical procedure ' *il fault prendre conseil selon l'opportunité du temps, des mœurs du peuple, et autres circonstances* '. The sixteenth century was not the first century ; God's providence had set the Church in new political surroundings, and the duty and aim of responsible Christians was, not to attempt so artificial a thing as an exact reproduction of the apostolic Church, but to reconstitute the Church in some form that would answer to the

apostolic standards of the Christian religion. Some
kind of government is needful for the order and effectiveness of the Church. But Calvin is careful to explain
(*Instit.*, IV. x. 30), ' since the Lord has not been pleased
to prescribe, in external discipline and ceremonies,
every detail which we are bound to follow (foreseeing
that this depended upon the nature of the times, and
declining to lay it down that one form should suit all
ages), here we must have recourse to the general rules
which He has given, using them to test whatsoever
the needs of the Church may require in the interests
of order and decorum. . . . Since matters of this kind
are not necessary to salvation, and since they ought
to be adjusted for the building up of the Church in a
variety of ways, answering to the customs of each age
and nation, it will be proper to change and abrogate
use and wont and also to institute new forms, as the
interests of the Church may require '. This is good
sense. But it was more easy to propound such a
view than to secure its realization. In course of time,
one must admit, when men of less breadth of mind
came upon the scene, the tendency was to regard the
New Testament too much as a book of authoritative
precedents and rules for ecclesiastical life ; in other
words, to slip into the error of using it as it was never
meant to be used. I say, the New Testament. For
although the Word of God was identified with the
whole Bible, for better and for worse, and while both
parties appealed to the Old Testament upon occasion,
the Episcopalians and Sacerdotalists to the Jewish
hierarchy as a precedent, and Presbyterian contro-
versialists to elders in the Israelitish Church as a
justification for lay-elders, the determining arguments

were naturally sought within the New Testament records. This proved a weakness sometimes. There was a risk, not always avoided, of undue rigour. Yet the result was a fairly common policy. In every quarter the Reformers of the Church spontaneously realized that a Presbyterian polity of some kind was more close than any other to the New Testament Church. The one exception to this rule was Luther. He had no objection to episcopacy as a form of Church government, provided that bishops would permit the Gospel to be preached. Luther was anxious to make as few changes as possible in the polity of the Church, and retained a modified form of bishops, though declining to confine ordination to them. He discouraged the attempt of the Reformers at Hesse to erect what was a Presbyterian polity on the lines of the apostolic Church, and preferred to make the episcopal authority and oversight work through consistorial courts, which, being appointed and regulated by the civil power, were only a far-off approach to presbyteries. There was a constitutional reason for this. In Germany princes supported the cause of the Reformers, and Luther was naturally unwilling to initiate any change in the polity of the Church which would conflict needlessly with the authorities. He was no jurist himself; indeed, he had a very small opinion of jurists in the Church. Fortunately there were Christian jurists, however.

In France, the new movement had the authorities before very long against it; the early hopes of episcopal aid were disappointed. Thus the Huguenots had then a free hand, and by 1555 they began to organize themselves on Presbyterian lines. The principles of their own Calvin appealed to the moral conscience and the sense of logical precision which lay in the French nature. Unable to carry on the episcopal system in any modified form, the Huguenots instinctively had recourse to Calvin's Presbyterian scheme based on the New Testament, with its three orders of minister, elders in a consistory, and deacons. Like the Scottish Church shortly afterwards, they drew up not only a Confession of Faith, but a Book of Discipline by the year 1559. The latter, as we shall see, had elements which influenced the Scottish polity. It was the French constitution which also came to mould the Reformed Churches in the Netherlands. As was only natural, for the Lutheran consistorial administration requires a friendly or sympathetic civil power, whereas ' Presbyterianism, as France, Scotland, and the Netherlands have proved, is the best suited for a " Church under the Cross ". Nor need this be wondered at, for the Presbyterian or Conciliar is the revival of the government of the Church of the early centuries while still under the ban of the Roman Empire '.[1]

Meantime Calvin had gone to Geneva, where the Syndics and Council had inaugurated their religious independence by choosing as the town motto ' Post tenebras lux '. He managed eventually to organize the local Church on a Presbyterian basis ; although he was thwarted and hampered by the civic authorities, he saw to the discipline of the Church being administered by presbyters and elders. The public enforcement of discipline in private life was a tradition of the mediæval civic life. What the Church now did, the Cantons had always done. ' Every instance quoted by modern historians to prove, as they think, Calvin's despotic

[1] T. M. Lindsay, *A History of the Reformation*, ii. 271.

interference with the details of private life, can be paralleled by references to the police-books of mediæval towns in the fifteenth and sixteenth centuries. To make them ground of accusation against Calvin is simply to plead ignorance of the whole municipal police of the later Middle Ages '.[1] Calvin found this discipline already enforced at Geneva, where it was needful, owing to the corruption of the local Roman Church. The morals of the citizens were the concern of the State, and it was Calvin's aim to see that the State, or rather the State Church of the municipality, carried out for the Church and with the Church the traditional ideals of civic discipline, in order to promote morals, education, and public welfare. The effect of it in Europe was startling. ' Government at Geneva was self-government mutually enforced by equals on each other. The power thus generated was too expansive to be confined to Geneva.' It spread and became a vital force in the reaction against a mediæval Christianity which ' had preached the base and demoralizing surrender of the individual, the surrender of his understanding to the Church, of his conscience to the priest, of his will to the prince '. It was the spirit of the French Calvin which taught Christians then to realize their true liberty without abusing it, to fight for it, if need be, against the autocracy of the Romanist powers. The Calvinistic discipline nerved men to prize and hold, at all costs, the essential freedom of Christians and the Church, when it was threatened alike by outside opposition and by internal individualism. ' This, and this alone, enabled the Reformation to make headway against the terrible repressive forces brought to bear by Spain—

[1] T. M. Lindsay, *A History of the Reformation*, ii. 108.

the Inquisition and the Jesuits. Sparta against Persia
was not such odds as Geneva against Spain. Calvinism
saved Europe.' So Mark Pattison, in his famous essay
on Calvin at Geneva. And by ' Calvinism ' he means
not simply a system of doctrine, but the Presbyterian
polity which made its beliefs about the Church an
effective force.

How effective it was, the struggle in the Netherlands
soon proved. As early as 1563 a Synod at Antwerp
had outlined a Presbyterian polity for which most of
the Protestants in the southern provinces longed, but
the brutal onset of the Spanish Romanists had to be
met and mastered before the Netherlands had any
opportunity of organizing their Church. When the
opportunity did come, there was serious trouble over
the relations of Church and State. In the end provincial Churches, all more or less Presbyterian, were
constituted, but there was no General Assembly for the
whole country. Then came the controversies over
Calvinism, which were fought out in the Dutch Presbyterian Churches more vigorously than in any other.
Secessions followed, as in the Scottish Church, and also
a partial reunion.   It is the acute tension between
orthodox Calvinism and liberalism which has characterized the Dutch Presbyterian Church throughout its
history ; the State question has also been a factor in
the struggles, but, to a far larger extent than in
Scotland or even than in Switzerland, it is doctrinal
differences that have come to the front.

Calvinism was also to inspire the Scottish people,
as we shall see in a moment. But before passing from
the Continent we may pause to notice an important
document which served to unite these early Churches

D

of the Reformation in a common Presbyterian, catholic alliance. I mean the Second Helvetic Confession. It was drawn up by one individual, and yet attained widespread international recognition. Henry Bullinger, Zwingli's successor at Zurich, compiled it in 1566, as a statement of the faith ' in harmony with the confession of the ancient apostolic orthodox Church, and likewise with all the faithful who with pure faith do profess Christ throughout the Churches of Germany, France, England, and other kingdoms and lands '. This was a large claim. But Bullinger had succeeded in voicing and expressing the beliefs of many Churches. In 1566 the Church of Scotland, for example, at once approved it ; so, before long, did the Churches in France and Hungary and Poland. It is a lengthy manifesto, in thirty chapters.[1]   But it had the double merit of raising Christian truth above the theological controversies of contemporary Switzerland, and also of presenting a resolute front to Roman theology as re-stated in the contemporary Roman Catechism of the Council of Trent. Until the Westminster Confession of Faith was drawn up, a century later, no more formidable counter-statement to the Roman claims held the field.

[1] The Latin original is reprinted in E. F. K. Müller's *Bekennt-nisschriften der reformierten Kirche* (1903), pp. 170–221.

CHAPTER IV

IN ENGLAND AND SCOTLAND

I

MEANTIME things were moving much less tragically and successfully in England. It is historically accurate to say that English Puritanism during the reign of Elizabeth was a movement inside the Church of England which sought to re-establish that Church on a Presbyterian basis.[1] Its protagonist was Dr. Thomas Cartwright, Lady Margaret Professor of Divinity at Cambridge since 1570. This learned scholar, in lecturing on the Acts of the Apostles, recognized that the constitution of the apostolic Church was Presbyterian. Cartwright had been a chaplain in Ireland, where he had come to sympathize with the party who disliked vestments and ceremonies ; now he went further, and created an academic sensation by proposing to re-constitute the Church of England on the primitive basis, abolishing archbishops and diocesan bishops, allowing each congregation to elect its own minister or presbyter, and so forth. When Whitgift, the Vice-Chancellor, afterwards Archbishop of Canterbury, had him at once deposed from his chair, he visited

[1] See Dr. Francis Paget's introduction to his edition of *The Fifth Book of Hooker's Ecclesiastical Polity* (Oxford, 1899).

Geneva, where he was deeply impressed by watching the Presbyterian polity in action. Then he returned to England, to enter upon a literary duel with Whitgift over the question of ecclesiastical polity. The controversy cut to the bone. For the first time the principles of Church government were debated in the light of Scripture. Whitgift and his opponent were both agreed, of course, that the Church did not require Scriptural warrant for every detail in her services and customs, and the Archbishop frankly allowed that Scripture ruled out the Mass and other Romanist errors. But Cartwright persisted that the Bible did prescribe a general polity for the Church which was Presbyterian, not prelatic. This Whitgift would not allow. Cartwright's argument was that the discipline and Prayer Book of the Church should be as free from Romanist elements as possible. That, on the negative side. On the positive, he maintained, for example, that Christ alone was Head of the Church, and that the civil magistrate or monarch was not exempt from spiritual discipline.

No one who is acquainted with the position and conduct of the bishops under Elizabeth can wonder that serious Christians saw little or nothing in diocesan episcopacy, as it was being worked in England, that recalled the apostolic Church. This radical movement of Cartwright and his allies raised some sympathy, especially in London and the neighbourhood. Indeed, on November 20, 1572, a presbytery, or (as we should now call it) a kirk-session, was constituted at Wandsworth; it was the first attempt to organize Presbyterianism in the country. But the Anglican authorities became alarmed at the spread and success of the pamphlets issued by Cartwright and his allies; the printing-press was stopped, and Cartwright, to avoid arrest, made his way to Heidelberg. This was in December 1573. He had been arguing with Whitgift for little more than a year and a half.

At Heidelberg, where the Presbyterian discipline was in full play, Cartwright breathed freely, till a Lutheran Elector arose to rule the Palatinate in 1576. Here, as afterwards at Antwerp, where he ministered to a local Presbyterian Church of English merchants, Cartwright became much less intolerant and narrow. Contact with the Brownist sectaries made him alive to the risks of a doctrinaire programme for the Church. He was still an ardent Presbyterian, but, hoping for a reform of the Church of England, he drew away from separatists who sharply disowned her. His hopes were not to be fulfilled. A beginning was indeed made. The exercises or conferences of clergymen held during Elizabeth's reign were meetings which practically corresponded to presbyteries. They were sometimes held monthly; their object was to bring clergymen together for discussion of religion, for mutual exhortation, and for the maintenance of Puritan interests throughout the country. In short, they were the inarticulate form of the later presbyteries. No wonder a rigid Anglican like Bancroft suspected that they were an adroit, subtle means of introducing the Presbyterian discipline into the Church, ' though they concealed the names, either of presbytery, elder, deacon, making little account of the name for the time, so that their offices might be secretly established '. A Book of Discipline was actually compiled in Latin : its English name was *A Directory of Church Government*. It provided for the reorganization of the English Church on Presbyterian lines, not on those of diocesan episcopacy, and a Bill to the same effect was introduced in the House of Commons in 1587. But the Queen and the bishops proved too much for the movement ; its connexion with the radical onslaught of the Marprelate Tracts did not help it ; and Dr. Cartwright himself was imprisoned in the Fleet and tried before the Court of the Star Chamber.

This was the first phase in England. The prospects of such a Presbyterian movement in the Church were much more favourable than the modern reader is apt to realize. In the light of the *fait accompli*, the attempt to re-shape the polity, revise the Prayer Book, and deal drastically with the ceremonies of the Church, appears more daring than feasible ; even had it been put forward in a less doctrinaire form, we are tempted to doubt whether it could have had any chance. Yet there was widespread support for it in influential quarters ; both at the Universities and in London it won ground. Nevertheless, Cartwright and his companions had not gauged the situation aright. For episcopacy had not only the prestige of tradition behind it, but the grateful support of the throne. It was part of the constitution, for one thing ; besides, the monarchy was indebted to it for past services. Ecclesiastics like bishops had been, by their personal ability and their freedom from feudal ties, one of the surest allies on which the new monarchies in England as well as in Spain and France had relied, in order to manage their affairs. Leading churchmen had aided kings to reign and rule, when there were few other persons in the State capable of rendering such excellent service. One drawback was that bishops were thereby diverted from their proper functions ;

churchmen as statesmen were neglecting their spiritual duties, or delegating them to subordinates, who were very imperfectly trained and inadequately supervised. The interest of bishops became divided, and this was brought up against them with startling effect at the Reformation ; much of the prejudice against prelacy and the hierarchy was due to the sharp sense of newly awakened religious people, that such high, haughty personages did not correspond in any obvious sense to what the New Testament laid down as ministerial or episcopal ideals. This prejudice was often voiced crudely and unfairly. Still, it was not unjustified, and it would have been more destructive than it proved to be, had it not been for the fact that the bishops had established their title to a secure place in the monarchical fabric. As a recent writer has put it,[1] ' When the Reformation had produced an educated laity, the churchmen could resume their proper duties, and bishops are as rare in Elizabeth's Privy Council as they are abundant in that of Henry VII. But the monarchy repaid their services by its support of the monarchical principle in the Church, and he would be a bold man who would assert that episcopacy would have survived as the governing principle of the Church of England had it not been for Tudor monarchy.'

Elizabeth as a statesman saw the imperative need of a national unity which implied Church unity, and as Church unity meant uniformity of worship and polity, the Presbyterian experiment had no chance. It smacked of a tendency which was subversive of authority. Essentially the government of the Church which the Presbyterian churchmen prepared was representative

In *The Times Literary Supplement* (January 10, 1918).

and constitutional, but it could readily be misstated, both by radical supporters and by outside critics, as though it were a plebeian ochlocracy, in which any so-called 'prophet' or group of self-styled spiritual persons, more or less illiterate, could claim to rule the parish. If it be true, as Dr. Scott Pearson suggests, that Presbyterian churchmanship was also compromised by its associations with Congregationalism, from which it was not always explicitly differentiated at this period, this may also help to account for the fact that during the latter part of Cartwright's career the sympathizers with his crusade 'were obliged to retain their Presbyterian principles in a state of suspended animation '.[1]

The one partial success of the period was won by foreigners for England. It was a rill from the tide of French Presbyterianism which flowed into the Channel Islands, and threw up a tenacious Presbyterian polity there, which Queen Elizabeth was induced to sanction. The Huguenot refugees had organized their consistories in Jersey by the year 1563, and in Guernsey it flourished, actually under the supervision of the Bishop of Winchester, for the Channel Islands, one of Britain's oldest possessions, were transferred to that see in 1569. The local governors fostered the movement loyally; both Poulet and Leighton had strong Puritan sympathies. Unluckily a quarrel between the two Island Churches checked this growth, and it was not until Dr. Cartwright took refuge in Guernsey, about 1595, that harmony was restored. Cartwright had failed in England, but he managed to make the Presbyterian discipline effective in Guernsey before he left in 1601 for Warwick. This

[1] *Thomas Cartwright and Elizabethan Puritanism*, p. 415. This is the best biography of the Cambridge scholar.

Presbyterian Church [1] had its vicissitudes, but it maintained itself even during and after the Civil War and the Restoration.

So ended the first phase of Presbyterianism within the English Church. But what Cartwright and his coadjutors failed to achieve, south of the Border, was achieved in the north by the resolute churchmen of Scotland.

II

Knox, like Calvin,[2] had no dogmatic objection to episcopacy as being unscriptural and sinful. What led the Scottish Church, through a series of early pronouncements marked by the *First* (1560) and the *Second* (1578) Books of Discipline, to draw up a rigid Presbyterian polity, was the position of the Church in relation to the State. Episcopacy was associated with features in the national life which were distasteful to many powerful interests in the Church and nation. The Scottish Reformation, for one thing, inherited an antipathy to the hierarchy, which had been growing throughout the country. The flower of the Scottish nobles had fallen on the field of Flodden,

> Where shiver'd was fair Scotland's spear,
> And broken was her shield.

The monarchy had perforce to fall back on the most competent men whom it could commandeer to carry

[1] There is a discussion of its organization in *The Transactions of the Congregational Historical Society* for May (1907), pp. 110–113.

[2] This is brought out for Calvin by M. J. Pannier in the *Revue d'Histoire et de Philosophie Religieuses* (1926), pp. 305–335.

on the State, and these were for the most part the
higher ecclesiastics. Thus during the reign of James V
the Roman clergy and their French supporters acquired
a predominant place in the administration of Scotland.
But by this time the glamour of the old alliance had
begun to fade; Scotsmen were asking themselves
whether it was worth while to keep up the old feud
with England. And when the Reformation came,
bringing the two countries into line in religion, patriotism
turned from attacking England to ousting the French
foreigners. From an important point of view, the
Reformation in Scotland turns out to be 'more than
a movement of ecclesiastical cleansing. It was a
patriotic outburst against the intrusion of foreigners,
whether civilian, uniformed, or frocked, in the affairs
of Scotland'. English help was needed and sought,
not always without risk. But the Romanists and the
agents of the Guises had to be got rid of at all costs.
'No doubt John Knox in one sense substituted tyranny
for tyranny, and his presbyter may often have been
but priest writ large. Still, the fact—so the Scot would
argue—that it was our own presbyter made all the
difference'.[1] More than that, the record of the Scottish
episcopacy was sorrowful. Rich properties of the
Church were held for gain's sake by men who had no
clerical character, and sometimes no character at all.
'At no time during the three hundred years which
preceded the Reformation does it appear that the
Scottish bishops succeeded in making orders an indispensable qualification for a benefice. . . . Rich livings,
with the care of thousands of souls, were held by boys,
by infants even, by men deformed in body, imbecile in

---

[1] *The Times Literary Supplement*, 1919, p. 53.

mind, hardened in ignorance, old in wickedness and sin.'[1] The best men in the Church had bewailed this, but it remained uncorrected. When the Reformation came, the new leaders of the Church determined that a system so careless of moral discipline and catholic order must go.

When the State authorities of Scotland in 1689 formulated their claim, abolishing prelacy, they urged ' that prelacy and the superiority of any office in the Church above presbyters is and hath been a great and insupportable grievance and trouble to this nation, and contrary to the inclinations of the generality of the people, ever since the Reformation, they having been reformed from popery by presbyters, and therefore ought to be abolished '. As abolished it was. This was not an untrue reading of history. Two bishops, indeed, joined the reforming cause, but the main impetus to the movement came from presbyters like the six John's, Knox, Row, Willock, Winram, Spottiswoode, and Douglas. The two bishops were time-serving prelates, in any case ; it was these six men who, at the request of Parliament, drew up the Confession of Faith in 1560, and provided for superintendents to organize the Church in various provinces or districts, under the General Assembly. Now prelacy is not the same as episcopacy. Prelacy, in *The Solemn League and Covenant* of 1643, is described as ' Church government by archbishops, bishops their chancellors and commissaries, deans and chapters, archdeacons, and all other ecclesiastical officers depending on that hierarchy.' This is not on all-fours with such an episcopacy as

[1] Joseph Robertson's preface (p. ccvi) to *Statuta Ecclesiæ Scoticanæ*.

men like Leighton would have set up. But episcopacy had a bad start in Scotland. Under James VI it was advocated by the monarch as a part of the constitution. The clergy were one of the Three Estates, and he naturally desired to carry on this arrangement, with some equivalent, at any rate, for the bishops. Besides, he had the sense to see that bishops were much more amenable to the throne than presbyters, who had the awkward habit of speaking their mind and of interfering, as James thought, arbitrarily with the policy of the State. Furthermore, he had to consider the Church of England. His heart was set on the English throne, and he desired to have a form of Church government in Scotland as uniform as possible with that of the southern Church, for the sake of unity. This was a laudable aim. Had it been feasible—and it might have been managed—it would have saved tears and trouble for all concerned. But episcopacy had been advocated by the civil authorities for quite unspiritual ends. There were bishops put into sees that their rich incomes might pass to the Crown, after the nominees had been allowed a small percentage. Such bishops were financial agents, devoid of any consecration or spiritual functions. The sharp-eyed Scottish churchmen resented episcopacy on these terms as an insult to the Church, and thus their leaders like Andrew Melville and Alexander Henderson had no sympathy whatever with any plea for episcopacy. James did manage to get episcopacy into the Scottish Church, but in a form which satisfied neither Episcopalians nor Presbyterians, for the presbyteries were still operative. The settlement, however, might have proved stable. What upset it was the absolutism of James and his son. Under Charles I the Scots rose to resent the royal prerogative exercised in matters ecclesiastical, and the result was a shrewd gust from the north in the seventeenth century which blew the bishops out of the Scottish Church and, for a time, out of the English Church as well. The tale of these eventful years and of their sequel for the Scottish Church may be read in Lord Balfour of Burleigh's *Rise and Development of Presbyterianism in Scotland*, which he contributed to the 'Cambridge Manuals of Science and Literature' in 1911, or in Sir Thomas Raleigh's posthumous *Annals of the Church in Scotland* (1921), which brings the story down to 1905.

So far as the internal shaping of Presbyterianism in Scotland went, during this period, i.e. down to about 1638, the dominant issue was the spiritual independence of the Church. It was this that really led to the reaction against episcopacy, for the latter was commonly, though unfairly, identified with the claims of the Crown to dictate the worship and polity of the Church. The sturdy, and even self-assertive defence set up by the Church was voiced by the Assembly. During the struggle of the Scottish Church against the policy of James VI and Charles I, the General Assembly 'represented the life, the genius, and the best interests of the Scottish people, and of Christianity itself, under the only form in which it could be a living faith *to them*. . . . Everything that was of value in any part of that contest, every hope of national life, every love of freedom, every desire of truth—in short, every upward tendency in human society was ranged on the side of Presbytery in Scotland, and was at stake with its success'.[1] What the House of Commons did for

[1] The Duke of Argyll in *Presbytery Examined*, p. 353.

England was done for Scotland by this great court of the Church, which, be it remembered, was not a clerical or ecclesiastical body. The General Assembly, as Professor Rait shows, 'made possible the existence of public opinion in Scotland, and the public opinion of Scotland was with the Assembly'.[1]

It is amusing to note the impression made by this Scottish Church as a real Church, acting independently within its province, upon a bishop like Dr. Bancroft in 1589. He denounces it as ' that counterfeit and falsely patched up government which is termed the Presbytery, a mere human device devised by shiftings and sleights, attained by tyranny and blood, and maintained with intolerable pride and with most strange boldness in expounding the Scriptures and falsifying of all antiquity '. This was much the same charge as that levelled by Presbyterian churchmen against prelacy. Yet both the English and the Scottish Churches at this period generally recognized one another as Churches. Indeed, the Church of England as yet recognized the Church of Scotland more freely than the latter sometimes recognized her sister. There is an odd proof of this in the 55th Canon, sanctioned by the Canterbury Convocation of 1603–4, where a bidding prayer, called ' The Form of a Prayer to be used by all Preachers before their Sermon ', exhorts the congregation to ' pray for Christ's holy catholic Church, that is, for the whole congregation of Christian prople dispersed throughout the whole world, and especially for the Churches of England, Scotland, and Ireland '. The Church of Scotland here is the Presbyterian Church of the day. There was no other Christian communion recognized as

[1] *The Scottish Parliament* (1901), p. 67.

such in Scotland.   It is certain that those who compiled
this Canon ' meant to acknowledge the northern ecclesiastical establishment as a Christian Church ; and such
was the opinion held by Bancroft and most of the
English prelates, although they believed the Scottish
system to be defective in its ritual, in the ordination of
its ministers, and in other points '.[1]

The organization of the polity, meantime, had been
slowly but surely beaten out.   In the *Second Book of
Discipline* (1578), which was practically ratified in
1592, the polity was outlined more fully than in Knox's
provisional arrangements, thanks to the constructive
statesmanship of Andrew Melville and his colleagues,
some of whom were acquainted at first hand with the
constitutional development of Presbyterian Churches on
the Continent.   Melville, especially, had come to know
intimately the spirit and the working of the Swiss
Churches during his residence at Geneva.   One of the
first results was that what the French Huguenots knew
as a Colloque, and the Churches of Swiss towns like
Lausanne and Berne as a Classe, became in the Scottish
Church a Presbytery.   There were differences, to be
sure.   The Presbytery, unlike the Colloque, did not
include deacons, and did exercise a disciplinary control
over the district congregations and their sessions.
Unlike the Swiss Classe, it did not consist merely of the
district magistrates and ministers, but of ministers and
representative elders.   Still, the court was now in
operation at last.   The function of presbyteries had
been recognized indeed by the English pioneer Cartwright ; in his scheme they are conferences or *colloquia*.

[1] Dr. Grub, *Ecclesiastical History of Scotland*, ii. 282.   Dr
Grub was a scholarly Episcopalian.

In the development of the Scottish Church they only emerged in the legislation of 1582 as a complete court. For the Scottish Church after the Reformation developed a constructive policy but slowly, and for a time presbyters had nothing between their kirk-session meetings every week and the half-yearly Synod. The superintendents really performed most of the duties that normally fall to a presbytery. But by 1580 the General Assembly began to prefer presbyteries to the limited autocracy of superintendents, and by 1590 the final step of creating presbyteries was taken.

So the office of superintendent waned before the rising sun of the presbytery. It had been an interesting experiment. The superintendent had discharged some of the functions which fall to a diocesan bishop, although strictly speaking he was no bishop. There is no sufficient evidence for the hypothesis [1] that the Church intended them to hold office until the bishoprics fell vacant. Once presbyteries were organized, a superintendent was soon felt to be superfluous; indeed, his office appears to have been a temporary makeshift—one of those special measures which a Presbyterian Church is free to make, in virtue of its flexibility, for some immediate ends of efficiency. But the most resolute Presbyterian may confess that in one respect a presbytery is less efficient than a single presbyter invested with episcopal (though not necessarily hierarchical) powers, and that is, in cases where a presbyter has to be dealt with for unbecoming conduct. The parity of presbyters may be good and true, but when a fellow-presbyter incurs some guilt, and a scandal has to be

[1] As stated by the late Professor Cooper in the *Christian Unity Association Papers* (1914), p. 394.

dealt with, there is a natural reluctance on the part of
his fellows to take action. Here a father in God has
an influence and authority, due to his position, which
gives him the right to move. He can deal on his own
initiative, privately and wisely, with the offender. I
am expressing more than a personal opinion when I
say that this seems to me to be one function of a bishop
which we as presbyters envy and admire. Discipline
of a presbyter by his fellows is often so painful and
delicate that it would be better carried out by one
like a superintendent. But we lost that when we lost
the superintendent's office in the sixteenth-century
development of the Church.

There had been precedents [1] in the Swiss and the
Lutheran Churches for the appointment of superintendents or visitors to supervise work throughout the
parishes. In Geneva their duties included preaching,
and it was as travelling preachers that Knox and Willock
had already served in this capacity under Edward VI
in the English Church. Such was one of the main
functions of the Scottish superintendent. He had not
only to see that ministers preached and fulfilled their
office generally, but he had to preach himself, at least
three times a week, besides examining ' the life, diligence,
and behaviour of the ministers, as also the order of
their Churches and the manners of the people ' in his
district or diocese.

But the office of superintendent is not the only
feature for which we must look abroad, in order to
understand the evolution of Scottish presbytery. Whilst
this development of Presbyterian government in Scot-

---

[1] See Richter's *Evangelischen Kirchenordnungen des XVI
Jahrhunderts* (1871), i. 173.

E

land was stimulated by national exigencies, the boards of elders, for example, being modelled on local burgh trade boards, it would be unjust to ignore the influence of the French Huguenots upon the Scottish Church in its formative period. Even in some verbal details it is evident. Thus the French ' moderateur ', which the Huguenots had taken over from the Gallican Church for their own ecclesiastical presidents, became the Scottish ' moderator '. Similarly, ' overture ', used in all ecclesiastical vocabulary both as a noun and as a verb, is from the French ' œuverture ', which opened vital pieces of business in the French assemblies.[1] But the influence went far deeper than words.

When we review the completed system, this stands out, that the Presbyterianism of the Scottish Church is not aggressively national or provincial. The very *munimenta* of its polity have been the work of Englishmen, the Confession of Faith, the Larger and the Shorter Catechisms, and the Directory for Publick Worship. Even the metrical Psalms, which have sung themselves into the heart of the people by their rugged strength and manly simplicity, go back to an Oxford man, a Provost of Eton. Half of the Scripture paraphrases and hymns are from Englishmen like Watts, Doddridge, Tate, and Addison. And, in particular, the administrative constitution of the Church was drawn up by men who were familiar with the practice of the French and the Swiss Churches, and who did not disdain to avail themselves of material which lay ready in the international situation of the Reformed Churches, in order to create their original polity for Scotland. The

[1] This was pointed out by Dr. Hill Burton in *The Scot Abroad* (ed. 1871), pp. 185, 186.

French precedents and parallels are noteworthy. At the Reformation the Scots threw off the foreign, French yoke from their national life. But by a curious paradox they were mightily indebted to France for the organization of their reformed Church. Recent research has disclosed ' the fact that, after 1560, the more elaborate system of courts which the growth of the Scottish Church necessitated developed largely along the lines laid down by the French Church in 1559 '.[1] Thus the Scottish General Assembly as a court of appeal, for example, corresponded more closely to the French Synods National than to any similar court even in the Genevan Church. Knox deeply admired the latter, as ' the most perfect school of Christ that ever was in the earth since the days of the apostles ', but he and his supporters worked out their polity in Scotland independently, as indeed they had to do, since the conditions were so different, drawing freely upon other foreign Churches for suggestions and precedents, following none blindly, but at the same time being alive to the most progressive elements in the international Presbyterianism of the day, such as those incorporated in the French *Discipline Ecclésiastique* of 1559. The main problem of the internal constitution was to reconcile the autonomy of the congregation with the efficient, corporate life of the larger Church. In Scotland the churchmen had to work this out for the first time upon a national scale, since there was no precedent either in the Swiss municipalities, much less in France, where between 1560 and 1578 the Church ' remained in the position of a proscribed and persecuted corporation, and was consequently

[1] Dr. Janet G. Macgregor, in *The Scottish Presbyterian Polity* (1926), p. 52.

unable to prove its theoretic polity by the touchstone of full application on a national scale '.[1] Melville and his coadjutors showed real statesmanship in their constructive programme. It completed the polity mainly by constituting the presbytery, which now linked the kirk-session to the General Assembly in a system that provided for freedom and order by this graduated series of courts exercising local, provincial, and central control of the Church's business. Neither in France nor even in Switzerland was it possible to show that Presbyterianism could develop a vital polity for the Church in national life. The opportunity of this fell to Scotland, and the passage of time proved that the Presbyterian constitution was as efficient and practicable as the episcopal in England ; in administrative self-government the Presbyterian polity indeed was second to none.

[1] *Op. cit.*, p. 117.

CHAPTER V

THE SEVENTEENTH CENTURY IN ENGLAND AND ITS SEQUEL

I

THE rising opposition to the autocracy of the King and the hierarchy in England during the first quarter of the seventeenth century led to a revival of Presbyterianism as the one constructive alternative to episcopacy. When the English Parliament undertook its responsibilities at the opening of the Civil War, it appealed to the Scots for aid. They, too, had been provoked by the King and the hierarchy of England; after Laud's untimely interference with their Church, they had reason to share any desire and plan for an ecclesiastical reform which would conserve popular liberty. To make a long story short, the Scots agreed to support their English allies, but upon one consideration: for the help of their army, they must receive an assurance that the Presbyterian polity be set up in England. This was granted, and Presbyterianism actually did become for a few years the official system, under the ægis of the House of Commons.

Even Milton paid a tribute to it, in his brief phase of sympathy with presbyteral ideas of polity and discipline. During the years 1641-2, when the nation was in its first flush of relief from the policy of Laud, when the Star Chamber had been stopped, and the hierarchy's autocracy had been curbed, it seemed wise to substitute presbyteral authority as a safeguard for Puritanism, and among the five pamphlets issued by Milton, one was a tract called ' The Reason of Church Government Urged Against Prelaty '. It contained this confession :—

So little do I fear lest any crookedness, any wrinkle or spot should be found in presbyterian government, that if Bodin, the famous French writer, though a papist, yet affirms that the commonwealth which maintains this discipline will certainly flourish in virtue and piety, I dare assure myself that every true protestant will admire the integrity, the uprightness, the divine and gracious purposes thereof, and even for the reason of it so coherent with the doctrine of the gospel, besides the evidence of command in scripture, will confess it to be the only true church government.

This word came from him in February 1642, after five Cambridge dons, Stephen Marshall of Emmanuel, Edmund Calamy of Pembroke, Thomas Young (who became Master of Jesus College), Matthew Newcomen of St. John's, and William Spurstow of St. Catherine's, had issued a notable pamphlet of Presbyterian principles. But the brief triumph of official Presbyterianism in England was due in the main to the political pressure on which the Presbyterian leaders at the Westminster Assembly could rely. The opponents of King Charles in England had tentatively agreed to the imposition of Presbyterianism as the sole form of worship and polity for England. A resolute argument against this was

tabled by the small group of Independents who claimed
freedom of worship and toleration of their particular
tenets. It was to reinforce such a claim that Milton
wrote his irregular sonnet on ' The New Forcers of
Conscience under the Parliament ', in which he now
defied the Presbyterian leaders to their face.

> Dare ye for this adjure the civil sword
> To force our consciences that Christ set free,
> And ride us with the classic hierarchy
> Taught ye by mere A. S. and Rutherford ?

A. S. was Dr. Adam Stewart, a Scotsman who was
professor first at Sedan and then at Leyden. He was
not a member of the Assembly, but came to London
and took part in the warfare of pamphlets which blazed
over the burning issue of Toleration. ' Rutherford ' is
Dr. Samuel Rutherford, Professor of Divinity in St.
Andrews University, that learned and saintly man who
wrote among other things *The Due Right of Presbyteries*,
The Divine Right of Church Government, and *A Free
Disputation against Pretended Liberty of Conscience*,
which made short work of any variations from Presbyterianism and invoked civil penalties upon any who
ventured to differ from Presbyterian doctrine and
discipline. Milton proceeds to uphold his new friends
the Independents :—

> Men, whose life, learning, faith, and pure intent
> Would have been held in high esteem with Paul,
> Must now be named and printed heretics
> By shallow Edwards and Scotch what d'ye call.

Edwards had already angered Milton by dubbing him
a heretic in his *Gangræna*, and the following term may
apply to Henderson, Gillespie, or Baillie, who with

Rutherford formed the Scots delegation to the Assembly. Probably Baillie was meant, since that Scotsman had publicly rebuked Milton for his easygoing views upon divorce.

The Presbyterian tyranny, of which Milton complained, was the reverse side of their beliefs about the Church. *'Tolle episcopos, et tot erunt schismata quot homines'* is the motto chosen by Sir Dudley Carleton for his *Testimonie concerning the Presbyterian Discipline in the Low Countries, and Episcopall Government here in England* (1642). His argument may command small agreement, but it is not difficult to understand his position, in an age when sects were beginning to swarm, and go-as-you-please, do-as-you-like, and think-what-you-choose seemed to be identified with free Christianity. To regard all non-episcopal religious life as anarchic was as just an estimate as the contemporary Calvinist's theory that any non-Calvinist belief, such as Arminianism, led to moral chaos and confusion. Yet it was intelligible. What Sir Dudley Carleton felt as an Episcopalian was felt by the Presbyterians themselves, as we may overhear them in the lament of Thomas Edwards. This good Presbyterian, convinced of the need for Church order and government, bewails in his *Gangræna* the licence into which liberty of speech and action in religious matters was slipping, and warns the House of Commons that England was in danger of ecclesiastical anarchy. 'You have made a Reformation, and blessed be God who put it into your hearts to do such things! but with the Reformation have we not a Deformation, and worse things come in upon us than ever we had before? . . . How do persons cast out of other countries for their errors, not only live here but gather churches, preach publicly their opinions ! What swarms are there of all sorts of illiterate and mechanic preachers, yes, of women and boy preachers ! What a number of meetings of sectaries in this city, eleven at least in one parish ! ' ' We have the plague of Egypt upon us, frogs coming out of the bottomless pit covering our land, coming into our houses, bedchambers, beds, churches ; a man can hardly come into any place, but some croaking frog or other will be coming up upon him.' A bitter cry. But it reveals one of the reasons why the Presbyterians then were so opposed to toleration. Such an antipathy was by no means confined to them ; still it puzzles us, till we recollect that in politics the idea of the homogeneous and all-authoritative State was dominant, as a really divine institution, while in religion (and religion was deeply woven into the political tissue) the conception of the visible, autonomous Church made the best of men eager to realize it in practice. Toleration of religious differences seems to us in modern days so axiomatic, that we are apt to misjudge those to whom in the seventeenth century it appeared a betrayal of truth and unity. Even yet it is not so simple as many people imagine to state a fair case for individual liberty of opinion. There are constantly emergencies when the theory has to be modified and abated, in the interests of the community. We may agree to-day, with Dr. Figgis, that ' from the Christian standpoint the great advantage of toleration is that it elevates automatically the life of the Church . . . it acts automatically on the purity of religious bodies and the reality of their faith ; and, where complete, it produces a temper which, annealed in the fires of constant criticism, is analogous to that produced by

persecution in the earlier days of the Church '.[1]   But
this philosophical attitude was unknown to the
ardent churchmen of the seventeenth century. Toleration to them was conniving at anarchy and condoning
error.

It was, again, reverence for Church-fellowship, and
especially for the sacraments, which made the zealous
Presbyterians, for example, insist on discipline as
essential to the living Church. They saw in English
diocesan episcopacy, as it was worked during the
seventeenth century, such carelessness about admitting
people to the Lord's Table, and such unspiritual procedure in Church courts on questions of excommunication, that they stressed the need for strict, real discipline,
such as the Presbyterian Church provided. 'Guard
the sacrament from scandalous and ignorant persons',
they claimed; 'catechize congregations, and have done
with the lax, parochial discipline of bishops and their
subordinates.' To which the bulk of the English
people for various reasons objected. The result was
that the Presbyterian polity and discipline failed to
establish themselves in the national life. Parishioners
in many cases refused to elect lay-elders, and the constitution of the presbyteries or *classes* remained ineffective, simply because the average English parishioner
resented what he regarded as a wanton interference
with his personal liberty. Discipline meant authority,
on the Presbyterian scheme, the authority of the Church
to regulate the behaviour of its members and to
scrutinize their religious opinions. But this seemed a
foreign intrusion, an invasion of private life by a new
kind of pope in the parish, as the English satirists were

---

[1] *Churches in the Modern State* (1913), pp. 118, 119.

never tired of crying, to the anger and astonishment of Presbyterians.

The Scottish Commissioners, in fact, had overrated the English feeling in favour of Presbyterian principles. It was true that in London and some English towns, in a few quarters like Cambridgeshire, Bedfordshire, and Lancashire, Puritan sympathizers both among the clergy and the laity of the English Church were not indisposed to alter episcopacy into the Presbyterian polity. But the Scottish Commissioners who had come down to England, as Dr. Masson puts it, like drill-sergeants to teach the English Presbyterians and others how to march in step and form themselves compactly, discovered before very long that they were up against a stubborn Erastian prejudice, and also against the congregational principles of the Independents, the latter party having Cromwell's disciplined army soon behind them.

The historical facts are familiar. Cromwell rose to power, with the Independents dominant in the army, and established a sort of tolerant Erastianism in England, for which not even his warmest admirer, to-day can summon up much enthusiasm. The Presbyterians in England and Scotland, as well as in Ireland-were tolerated, but their effectiveness and self-government were hampered. In one way, they handicapped themselves by adhering to the Scottish Covenants. In another, and a more honourable way, they were handicapped by their steady refusal to become republican. The former profited them nothing. For the latter they hoped to be rewarded at the Restoration, but, as it turned out, their hopes were vain. They put their trust in a prince, and they were confounded, both in

England and in Scotland and Ireland, but worst of all in England.

Still, this has to be said. It is true that Presbyterians in the seventeenth century did wish to have a single form of Church government for both England and Scotland, and to insist upon uniformity, just as Laud and Charles wished to make a uniform system for both countries on liturgical and hierarchical lines. But there was a difference between the two projects. The Scotsmen desired that the Form be drawn up and adopted by the nations or Churches themselves, acting through their representatives. This was the idea underlying the Westminster Assembly. Whereas Laud and Charles never consulted the Scottish Church, when they sought to impose their will upon its worship; the alteration was thrust on the Church by an act of autocratic power. And this was alien to the spirit of the Presbyterian Church, which as a true Church claimed the right of self-government. Let it be granted that the Presbyterians did not eschew coercive measures upon occasion in order to achieve their ends. Still, their principle was not ' uniformity dictated by one Church to another '. Technically they were willing and ready to have their plan discussed openly and details adjusted. If they imagined that episcopacy was no longer a vital issue, since it had been formally abolished by the King and Parliament, that was a grievous error of judgment. If they also imagined that the English people were, like themselves, a coherent, self-governing community, with a real interest in religious unity and uniformity, that again was an illusion, for which they were to pay dearly in the end. But, while both parties in their day of power, the Presbyterian and the prelatic, sacri-

ficed far too much to the insensate passion for uniformity
of worship in the realm, the Presbyterian methods were
not quite on all fours with those of their opponents.
The result for both parties was to be the same : authority
in one country and the position of a small minority in
the other. As it fell out, Presbyterianism and episcopacy were to appeal to the traditions and temperament
of the countries north and south of the Border respec-
tively. But at the moment no one could be expected
to foresee that the settlement of the swaying problem
would be reached in this direction. Each party had
its eyes bent upon a domination of the whole country
governed by the King, and the main distinction between
the two, as far as ecclesiastical methods went, was
that the Presbyterians sought to effect their purpose
by constitutional Church means, not by an arbitrary
use of authority. We are amazed to-day at the guile-
lessness of so astute a man as Alexander Henderson,
the great Scottish leader, who thought that to sweep
away prelacy and substitute Presbyterianism in the
English Church was a ' pious and profitable work ',
which ' without forcing of conscience seemeth not only
to be possible but an easy work '. This calm assurance
of the divine right of Presbyterianism, and of the
disposition of the English people to throw episcopacy
overboard, is staggering to us, who look back upon
the situation in the light of its sequel. But the words
' without forcing of conscience ' are notable and
honourable. Nor are they a casual phrase. In their
best moments the leaders of the Presbyterian propaganda were true to this principle. Thus George Gillespie,
preaching before the House of Commons, declared,
' When I speak against liberty of conscience, it is far

from my meaning to advise any rigorous or violent course against such as, being sound in the faith, holy in life, and not of a turbulent or factious carriage [behaviour], do differ in smaller matters from the common rule. " Let that day be darkness, let not God regard it from above, neither let the light shine upon it ", in which it shall be said that the children of God in Britain are enemies and persecutors of each other.' But such was not the impression made upon the English nation, and a Church suffers as it rouses against itself the best public opinion of the day. Even in 1643 good Mr. Robert Baillie wrote from London that ' as yet a Presbyterie to this people is conceived to be a strange monster '. It seemed as monstrous, twenty years later, after the English people had had a closer acquaintance with it, nearly as monstrous as prelacy seemed to the Scots.

Probably the reasons for the failure of Presbyterianism to attract England go farther back still. In England the re-formation of the Church was carried out for the people, whereas in Scotland it was the spontaneous action of the people, priests of the Church and devout laity rising to inaugurate and consolidate a religious movement of their own against the wishes of the Throne. This made the Scots far more interested in their Church as a religious community ; it trained the body and bulk of the nation to take some intelligent part in the working of the Church, till Presbyterianism, with its courts, and especially with its General Assembly, had become natural for a people who took to self-government in the religious as well as in the political sphere.

II

Again, Presbyterianism had failed to root itself within the Church of England. The second effort had been backed by a coalition between the English and the Scots. For the latter the check was a blessing in disguise ; it threw them back upon themselves, led them to realize slowly the meaning and limitations of their Church principles, forced them into more constitutional ways, and finally resulted in the triumphant settlement of the Presbyterian Church as the Church of Scotland. For the English Presbyterians the issue was much less happy, as we must now pause to notice.

The enforcement of the Clarendon code after the Restoration proved disastrous to the Presbyterian cause in England. There were individual ministers who managed to live usefully and happily, like the great Bible Commentator, Matthew Henry (1662–1714), in the second generation, whose dying testimony was that 'a life spent in the service of God and communion with Him is the most pleasant life that anyone can live in this world'. Henry's saintly and scholarly character shone out in his long ministries at Chester and London. But while he and others like him were distinguished for their personal qualities, the larger cause which they served was crumbling away under their feet. For the time being all that Presbyterian churchmen could say to one another was '*Durate, et vosmet rebus servate secundis.*' It is true that a month or two after the Act of Uniformity, Mr. Pepys reports a strong feeling still in favour of the Presbyterians among some London circles. 'The towne . . .

as far as I can hear will never be contented with Episcopacy, they are so cruelly set for Presbytery, and the
Bishopps carry themselves so high, that they are never
likely to gain anything upon them ' (November 10,
1662). But episcopacy won its way, even in London.
Individual bishops might be overbearing, and there
might be a dull popular resentment against the ecclesiastical courts and against the secular associations of
the hierarchy with the Crown ; but there was no statesman on the English bench of bishops to restrain the
vindictive policy which swept the country. Scott
makes you feel it in the pages of *Peveril of the Peak.*
The Presbyterians were now treated with the same
harshness as they had dealt out to the Episcopalians.
As time went on, they were forced into the position of
a sect, and, to make matters worse, they disintegrated
into Arianism and Socinianism during the eighteenth
century.

Various reasons have been given for this lapse of so
many Presbyterian congregations. They were certainly
handicapped by the impossibility of organizing themselves adequately. Presbyterial supervision over the
orthodoxy of ministers was next to impracticable ;
there was a mistaken aversion to tests and credal
subscription on the part of ministers ; and the Church,
excluded from the Universities by law, had insufficient
control over the academies in which candidates for the
ministry were trained. Local and wealthy trustees also
came to have more power in many congregations than
the presbytery, for by law religious property outside
the Anglican Church had to be held by trustees, and
wealthier congregations seem to have attracted ministers
of the Arianizing type. It is true that this ' Arian '

movement affected the Church of England as well.[1]
Both the archbishops, Warburton and Herring, were
sympathizers with the liberalizing desire to relax or
to abolish subscription to credal formulas and to
reinterpret Christian dogmas. But the Presbyterian
Churches were so hampered by civil restrictions that
their order and government failed to enforce itself. A
number of Churches thus fell away, remaining Presbyterian in name alone. Colonel Maurice explains this in
the biography of his father [2] as due mainly to the
reaction against creeds, which made these Presbyterians
now repudiate subscription to the Westminster Confession or to any other formula. The truth was that
as the Presbyterian Church hospitably welcomed anyone,
apart from adherence to any creed, ' all those who
found themselves unable to subscribe to the formulae
required by other denominations flocked towards Presbyterianism. Notably those who refused to subscribe
to the belief in the Trinity, and who were therefore
ejected by the most tolerant of all other bodies, fled
to Presbyterianism as to the one haven open to them '.
Naturally they included some of the ablest leaders in
the new science and philosophy, but these ' new apostles
who joined it from without, and of whom two notably,
Priestley and Belsham, formed and all but formulated
for it a creed, were men of vehement assertion and
scarcely disguised contemptuous aggression against all
who differed from a pure Unitarianism '.

Still a small nucleus was left, and for them a revival

[1] The best account of all this has been given by Mr. J. Hay
Colligan in *The Arian Movement in England* (1913) and
Eighteenth Century Nonconformity (1915).

[2] *Life of Frederick Denison Maurice*, i. 1-6. Maurice's father
was a Unitarian of this ' Presbyterian ' type.

F

of real Presbyterianism came through the influence of the Scottish Church. The 'Arianizing' movement had indeed affected that Church as well; but the Scottish Church was too well organized to crumble away, it had the Westminster standards as a safeguard, and the good of the liberal movement was assimilated eventually, although not without severe controversy. Its Scottish sympathizers are among the 'New Lights' to whom Burns refers in his poems. Professor Simson of Glasgow University was the chief supporter who was dealt with by the General Assembly, and it was ministers who had been trained in Glasgow University, where they had imbibed a liberal antipathy to traditional Calvinism, who led the progressive movement within the Ulster Presbyterian Church, from 1705 onwards. Eventually these non-subscribers to the Creed became the Unitarians in Ireland, as in England. One result of the Irish trouble was that the Church in 1785 started a theological college of its own, lest its students should incur further heterodoxy by attending, as heretofore, the University of Glasgow. But the Scottish Church maintained its credal orthodoxy as a Church, and it was immigrants from Scotland who rekindled genuine Presbyterianism south of the Border. They brought with them variant traditions. Some were from the Church of Scotland, more from the seceding bodies. Since 1851 the few surviving congregations of the former have been constituted 'The Scottish Synod in England in connection with the Church of Scotland'. The latter, since 1876, have been 'The Presbyterian Church of England', with about 350 congregations and 85,000 communicants.

Before leaving this phase, I mention two things:—

(a) These fortunes or misfortunes of Presbyterianism

in England account for a good deal. They explain, for example, the English ignorance and uncertainty about Presbyterians, which George Eliot amusingly describes in the first chapter of *Janet's Repentance*. In the Red Lion Inn some village worthies are discussing the Church ; there are Mr. Dempster the local lawyer, Mr. Tomlinson a rich miller, and Mr. Luke Byles, who observes, ' " In point of fact, these Evangelicals are not Churchmen at all; they're no better than Presbyterians." " Presbyterians ? what are they ? " inquired Mr. Tomlinson. . . . " The Presbyterians ", said Mr. Dempster . . . " are a sect founded in the reign of Charles I, by a man named John Presbyter, who hatched all the brood of Dissenting vermin that crawl about in dirty alleys, and circumvent the lord of the manor in order to get a few yards of ground for their pigeon-house conventicles." " No, no, Dempster ", said Mr. Luke Byles, " you're out there. Presbyterianism is derived from the word presbyter, meaning an elder." " Don't contradict *me*, sir ", stormed Dempster. " I say the word Presbyterian is derived from John Presbyter, a miserable fanatic who wore a suit of leather, and went about from town to village, and from village to hamlet, inoculating the vulgar with the asinine virus of Dissent." " Come, Byles, that seems a deal more likely ", said Mr. Tomlinson, in a conciliatory tone, apparently of opinion that history was a process of ingenious guessing.' Mr. Dempster seems to have confused the Presbyterians with the Quakers. But the point is that such ignorance and contempt for Presbyterians as mere dissenters is just as intelligible as the tone of the allusions to them in English literature. From *Hudibras* to Swift and Walpole, the references are unusually irritable and scornful. *Hudibras* reflects the impression made by the seventeenth-century attempt upon England ; Swift's pique is due to the friction between Episcopalians and Presbyterians in Ireland ; and Walpole's disparaging comments, like Dr. Johnson's, belong to a class which was stirred by the plight of the Presbyterians which has been already described.

(*b*) But the eighteenth century saw the rise of Presbyterianism in another quarter of the country. It might dwindle in England, yet in Wales it sprang into life under the evangelical renaissance which began by promoting ' societies ' for the growth of spiritual fellowship among members of the State Church. The revival movement started by Howell Harris in 1735 took Presbyterian form in 1811. Thus the Calvinistic Methodist Church is a Presbyterian body, though the function of the Assembly does not yet correspond to that recognized in other Presbyterian Churches ; the administrative powers remain with the two Synods or Associations of North and South Wales. In 1925 there were nearly 1,500 congregations, with close upon 189,000 Church members or communicants. The Church is predominantly Welsh in language and spirit.

CHAPTER VI

THE SPREAD AND EXPANSION

I

WITHIN Europe the seventeenth century had other and happier *sequelæ* for the Presbyterian Churches. These were partly due to the consolidation of Presbyterianism upon a sounder basis, and partly to the scattering and re-distribution of nations. Both of these factors emerge in Scotland.

While Wales, as we have seen, owed her Presbyterian movement to England, Ireland had already received it as an overflow from Scotland. By the first quarter of the seventeenth century Scottish Presbyterians were passing across into the north of Ireland, where King James was planting Ulster. The King was against Puritans and Presbyterians at home, but he was not unwilling to grant them concessions of land, that the north of Ireland might be civilized and developed. Among the settlers were a number of farmers from Ayrshire and Wigtonshire especially, who brought over ministers of a high type. It seemed to many that there was more freedom in Ulster than in their own country, where prelacy was being forced upon the people. Such was the start of the Presbyterian Church in Ireland. Under the Commonwealth it suffered, for the members could not welcome Cromwell's tolerant scheme for some loose, semi-secular organization of preaching stations. Such was not to their mind the Church of God. They clung also with obstinacy to the Covenants, which appeared irritating and disloyal to the Republicans. And their hardships did not end with the Restoration by any means.

There were, of course, Presbyterians in the south. The first Provost of Trinity College in Dublin, Dr. Travers, had been a Presbyterian. But the few Presbyterians in the southern part of the country were English by tradition, and apt, from their isolated situation, to be more congregational in polity than their northern brethren. On both the reactionary policy of the English after the Restoration fell heavily. Even after the Revolution the northern Presbyterians did not gain much by their loyalty, and the friction with the episcopal Church continued. Swift, for example, seems to have regarded the Presbyterians as the most dangerous and obnoxious rivals of his own Church. He spurted venom upon them. And his spirit was not uncommon, after the tolerant policy of Ussher had been checked. Bitterness grew on both sides. It was not until the beginning of the eighteenth century that political relief was tardily granted to the Presbyterians, and even then it was incomplete. One sad result was that many emigrated to America, carrying with them memories of tyranny associated with English rule and episcopal authority. And this in course of time worked against the English in America, for these settlers and their descendants sided ardently with the revolutionary cause, having learned to know in a hard school what were the merits of representative government and where the worst menace to it lay.

At home the Scots, like the English and the Irish, had to get through the Commonwealth régime and the Restoration reaction, disappointed but resolute. What distinguished their fortunes was that they were, as neither of the others was, the Church of the land. The following years are a series of family quarrels and reconciliations : three secessions, in 1732, in 1752, and finally in 1843. But in every case the trouble arose over the question of the State's relation to the Church. A theological issue was mixed up indeed with the Secession of 1732, but primarily all the divisions were ecclesiastical, in the sense that the parties who left the Church maintained they were carrying on the true idea of the Church as free and national. As Carlyle acutely observed, ' All Dissent in Scotland is merely a stricter adherence to the National Kirk at all points.' It was, essentially, although not all the seceding bodies remained true to the principle with which they started out.

Under Charles II and his successor, the Scottish Church had to encounter the imposition of an Erastian episcopacy, worked by the Earls of Rothes, Middleton, and Lauderdale, with James Sharp of St. Andrews as their clerical abettor. Again episcopacy came before the nation with the most compromising associations. Had moderation and wisdom been shown by the King and his English advisers, there might have been a fair chance of some permanent settlement. Outwardly there was barely any difference between Episcopalian and Presbyterian worship ; neither ceremonies nor liturgy were used, and even when the English Prayer Book was eventually introduced, it was not welcomed heartily. The episcopal functions were limited, and

many moderate men would have been glad to work
for some harmonious understanding. But the ruthless
policy of the Crown's agents wrecked the prospects of
a better time, long before the bishops finally discounted
their party by committing it to Jacobitism. In 1662
curates were beginning to be intruded into parishes
against the will of the people, and this was accompanied in the West particularly by military measures
which corresponded to the dreadful dragonnades in
France. The heroic, tragic episode of the Covenanting
struggle followed. 'We may safely hope', with Sir
Walter Scott (in the first chapter of *Old Mortality*),
'that the souls of the brave and sincere on either side
have long looked down with surprise and pity upon
the ill-appreciated motives which caused their mutual
hatred and hostility, while in this valley of darkness,
blood, and tears.' The fanaticism of the Killing Time
left its immediate effects upon the temper of the nation,
however. The responsibility for the turmoil over the
grievances felt by the extremists lay with the agents
of the Government, and the bishops and their supporters shared the odium. When the Revolution came,
the settlement of the Church was managed wisely ; the
ultra-Presbyterian intolerance was dropped, and the
Church was now based upon a sounder ground in
relation to the State. For which the chief credit is
due to the statesmanship of William Carstares, who
afterwards became Principal of the University of
Edinburgh. He was a trusted adviser of King William,
the man for the hour, as it proved ; indeed, Lord
Rosebery's deliberate opinion is that he was 'perhaps
the greatest man that Scotland has produced outside
literature '. Thanks to his sagacity, the negotiations

were steered clear of extremes on both sides. The Presbyterian government was enacted now for the Church, not on any basis of *jus divinum*, which would have involved persecuting methods alien to King William, but as ' agreeable to the Word of God ', and as, since 1592, ' received by the general consent of this nation, to be the only government of Christ's Church within this kingdom '.

There was harshness in the ejection of the curates. It might indeed seem that during the seventeenth century the Presbyterians in Scotland were either oppressed or oppressing. And in some of their declarations at and after the Revolution settlement the old intolerant spirit burst out. Yet, in practice, the Presbyterians were better than their word. Their dislike and repudiation of Toleration is indefensible, from a modern point of view, even although it may be historically intelligible. Yet they did not act upon their principles of intolerance, even when they had the power in their hands. Let that be said of them, in all fairness. And it has been said. Dr. John Hill Burton, who traces the intolerant spirit of the Scottish churchmen to Huguenot influences, allows that the wild Whigs of the West did not use the Revolution as the Huguenots would have done. ' Scarcely any religious body has lifted up more intolerant testimonies than the Covenanters, yet it would be difficult to point to any other large communion—save the Church of England—with fewer stains of blood upon it than Presbyterianism in Scotland.'[1] We may accept this verdict, although it must be added that what helped to restrain vindictiveness was the determination of the

[1] *The Scot Abroad* (ed. 1897), p. 186.

King and the Church's best leaders to effect a settlement which should make for national unity and
peace.

The fanatical feeling smouldered, but it was best
allowed to die down and to die out of the country,
under the larger interests of Christian missions and
propaganda.   Unluckily in 1712 the English Parliament
passed an Act restoring lay patronage in the Church
of Scotland, a measure due to the desire of the Jacobites
and the Tories to have the clergy more under the control
of the landed gentry.   This in the long run bred bitter
misunderstanding.   It raised the question of the freedom of congregations to choose their own ministers,
or at least to have a say in that procedure of the Church.
Those who held that it involved an infringement of
the true rights of the Church put their case in the
vivid Scottish phrase, 'The Crown Rights of Christ in
His Church'.   In 1843 the Free Church parted from
the Church of Scotland because it considered that the
liberties of the Church were infringed by the attitude
of the State towards the national Church over this
point, so sensitive were they upon the right of the
Church to self-government.   The Free Churchmen
claimed that 'in all matters touching the doctrine,
discipline, and government of the Church, her judica-
tories possessed an exclusive jurisdiction founded on
the Word of God, which power ecclesiastical flows
immediately from God and the Mediator, the Lord
Jesus Christ'.

It was hoped that a reunion of the Presbyterian
Churches in Scotland would be rendered feasible, when
the handicap and obstacle of patronage was removed
by the State in 1874, and the larger issue of self-

government decided in favour of the Church. This reunion is now in sight. But the promise of a lasting settlement has not been won without the pain of self-sacrifice or without clear and keen argument upon the principles of the Church. The Scottish Churches are at last attaining a solution of the vexed problem of Church and State, such as no other country has witnessed. This would not have been possible had not the members of the Scottish Churches been true to their convictions with an intelligent and passionate loyalty. Much has been learned both by the State and the Church since 1712 and 1843, but the Church has taught the State one thing, in the course of educating its own people, that the Church is neither an arbitrary theocracy nor a mere department of the State, but organized as a self-governing communion which is finally responsible to her Head and Lord. It has been Presbyterianism which rendered this solution possible and made it a success. In the Scottish Churches the members act together through representative courts, with a corporate and constitutional action. They are not a party which is a law to itself in a loosely organized religious society. Comparisons are sometimes odious, but there is a time and place for comparisons, in the interests of knowledge, and at this point I quote Professor Carnegie Simpson's expert opinion on the radical difference between the Churches of Scotland and England. ' The Scots high churchman, despite his fanaticism, which even led him into disruption for his principles, was never anarchic, but was strictly constitutional; while the Anglican high clericalist has really lost all sense of constitutionalism, and has made the whole idea of law and order within the Anglican Church no better than a farce.

In other words, the Scots churchman has stood by and *has achieved* liberty ; the Anglican clericalist *has taken liberties* ! The two things are not quite the same '.[1]

To conclude. The issue finally raised at the disruption of 1843 has now been settled satisfactorily, and the Church of Scotland will soon be one again, so ' United ' and ' Free ' that no section of its members requires these adjectives any longer as a distinctive title. Generosity and good feeling on the part of both Churches, a statesmanlike policy on the part of the responsible leaders, the co-operation of the State, and— it must be added—a driving impetus from the elders and people, have contributed to this happy prospect.

What these three centuries in Scotland have done for Presbyterianism, therefore, has mainly been to elucidate in terms of modern thought and practice the dominant conception of the Church. The exigencies of the situation have led to this being defined in relation to the State, with a success to which there is no parallel in any other country. But the central idea underneath the long, painful struggle, when misconceptions often swayed both sides, and when a synthesis seemed sometimes impossible under the clashing of sharply drawn antitheses, was the Presbyterian belief in the Church as at once a divine institution, with freedom to govern itself, and also as the Church of the nation, with relations and responsibilities to the State.

Before turning to this cardinal doctrine of the Church, we must survey rapidly the remarkable expansion of the Presbyterian Churches outside Scotland since the seventeenth century.

[1] *The Review of the Churches*, January (1926), p. 74.

II

The French Churches meantime were faring much like the Scottish, although they did not come through the struggle to any national success. The Huguenots were suffering from the dragonnades at the same time as the Scottish Covenanters. But the Revolution of the Edict of Nantes was a blow from which they never recovered. The eighteenth century witnessed a tenacious resistance, inspired from 1715 onwards by Antoine Court; the Church of the Desert held its ground till the Revolution, but under the Napoleonic era the Presbyterian Synods could not become effective, and it was not until 1848 that a Synod at Paris organized Presbyterianism. At once friction arose over the clash between orthodox and liberal theologies. The secession, under F. Monod, resembled that of the Free Church of Scotland in 1843, except that it was inspired by a credal controversy. It is the tension between the traditional Calvinism and the liberal Christianity of the age which has marked the French Churches ever since. There are shining names, like that of Coillard in foreign missions, D'Aubigné, Monod, Guizot, Doumergue, Coquerel, Bersier, Sabatier, and Roberty, and a host of others, in literature, theology, and the pulpit; but numerically the French Churches to-day muster only about 120,000 communicants, and the Reformed Church of Alsace and Lorraine, added since the Great War, is still small, only about 50,000 souls. Yet, as Bersier proudly claimed in 1888, their poverty has been the riches of many nations, and their contribution to Biblical criticism, especially of the liberal type, is to be remembered with gratitude.

The Swiss Churches, during the nineteenth century, suffered also from secessions due to the evangelical spirit, which in Vaud under Vinet, in Geneva under Malan, and in Neuchâtel under Godet, broke with what these leaders considered to be the Erastianism of the Cantonal Churches. Theology and foreign missions did not suffer, however, and now there is a Federation which includes almost all the evangelical Churches of the country, with responsibilities for two and a half million people.

During the seventeenth century the Bohemian *Unitas Fratrum*, which since 1496 had introduced into its Presbyterian system the interesting office of a bishop elected by and for each synod, was shattered by Romanist persecution. Eventually it revived in the nineteenth century, although even after 1861 its Presbyterian organization was thwarted by the State. The rise of Czecho-Slovakia, since the Great War, has witnessed an extraordinary break-away from the Roman Church, with the result that there is now an evangelical Church of Czech Brethren, adhering to the Hussite, Bohemian traditions, organized on Presbyterian lines, and numbering already a quarter of a million adherents.

Hungary's Presbyterian Churches go back to the sixteenth century, when they flourished particularly in Transylvania. Owing to the political stress, the seventeenth century proved for them a long, evil hour, but they emerged stronger than ever in the end of the eighteenth century. *Nec tamen consumebatur.* Again, as in Bohemia, recourse was had to episcopal superintendents, for the sake of efficient organization. The political re-arrangement of Central Europe after the Great War, with the break-up of Austro-Hungary, wa hard upon the Church. There are now no fewer than four segments of what is called the Magyar Reformed Church ; the largest and strongest, in Hungary, includes over a million and a half souls, in Transylvania and other parts of Rumania there are about 720,000, with 210,000 in Czecho-Slovakia and Ruthenia, and about 60,000 in Jugo-Slavia, where the political difficulties are still a menace. There is also at Vienna a small superintendency of the Reformed Helvetic Church.

As for Germany, under the Reformirte Bund of 1884, there are evangelical, reformed Churches with the Presbyterian polity in Prussia, Hanover, and Lippe, responsible for over 600,000 souls.

Far more notable has been the development in the Netherlands. The close connexion of Holland and Scotland during the seventeenth century made the Presbyterian refugees seek sanctuary often in the Netherlands. The rigid policy of the Romanist authorities in France had diverted Scottish adventurers in thought and scholarship from France to the more free and sympathetic republic of Holland ; the great Universities of Leyden and Utrecht now attracted students, as Paris and Bordeaux once had done. More than that, during the persecution in England and Scotland, Puritans and Scottish emigrants sheltered freely in the Low Countries, where the Presbyterians had their kirks and sessions. Yet Scotland never affected the course of things in the Netherlands, where local conditions created a special set of problems. In the Netherlands, as in Scotland, the Church, from 1571 onwards, was face to face with the problem of adjusting its relations to the State, so as to secure spiritual freedom and effectiveness. Troubles over Church government caused friction and division repeatedly, as at Haarlem ; one party desired the civil authorities to have control over the Church in the interests of order and amity, while the stricter Calvinistic Presbyterians upheld the autonomy of the Church. The bitter separations that have torn the Churches of the Netherlands sprang from a mixture of theological and ecclesiastical differences, from the Synod of Dort in 1618 onwards.[1] Liberalism or rationalism has clashed with Calvinistic orthodoxy, and the divergence has been accentuated by a sharp cleavage over spiritual independence. What the small body of the Remonstrants resented was often the inquisitorial discipline of Church courts no less than the severe Calvinism of the creed. At present, ' Die Groote Kerk', or the National Church, and the younger union of the secession Churches, called ' The Reformed Churches of the Netherlands ' (since 1892), number between them over two thousand ministers, and claim a membership of well over a million. But their past has been stormy. In the nineteenth century trouble arose over the question of State and Church, combined with doctrinal disputes, which led to a couple of secessions, the first in 1837, which threw up later the vigorous personality of Bavinck, the second in 1886 under the auspices of Dr. Abraham Kuyper, the outstanding figure of political and religious life during last century in the Netherlands. However, both secessions joined in 1892, although the two great Churches of the country, established and dissenting, have not yet come so close together as in Scotland.

[1] George Gillespie, in his book on the government of the Church, called *Aaron's Rod Blossoming* (Book ii. ch. 1), declared that ' the tutor which bred up the Erastian error was Arminianism '.

Belgium, in the south of the Netherlands, had suffered heavily under Alva's ruthless measures, and only revived its Presbyterian Churches in the nineteenth century ; they include about fifty staunch but struggling congregations.   Islets of Presbyterianism are also to be found in Denmark, Norway (where, as in America, the Evangelical Free Church is Presbyterian in polity, though Lutheran in theology), Greece, Bentheim and East Friesland, Galicia, Warsaw, Spain, and Lithuania. There the Churches are *rari nantes in gurgite vasto.* And to these falls to be added the Waldensian Church in Italy.

III

From the seventeenth century onwards there was a steady spread of the Presbyterian Churches, as the world outside Europe opened up.   (*a*) Emigrants to the New World across the Atlantic took their Presbyterian faith with them, and the home Churches followed them up by granting both men and money.   The same was true of the Dutch and the Scots in the Far East and under the southern stars.   These colonists remained Presbyterians.   (*b*) Finally, when foreign missions started, the Presbyterian Churches naturally tended to organize their converts on the lines of the home Church, particularly when this suited some of the local needs of a mission.   In these and in other ways a remarkable expansion has taken place.   Presbyterianism proved itself often a strong suitable form of organization ; it did not leave minister and congregations to themselves with no great Church to back them up.   It could undertake propaganda and initiate mission enterprise on a scale impossible for less well-knit Churches.

G

(a) The Huguenot exiles from France, who sought refuge in America during the latter half of the sixteenth century, were the first Presbyterian Christians in that continent. Englishmen followed; indeed, the original settlers in Virginia seem to have included some convinced Presbyterians. Then came the seventeenth-century emigration to New England from Holland and England; the Dutch Reformed Church started in New York in 1628.[1] The colonists who, after 1620, landed on Massachusetts Bay were 'for the most part either Presbyterian, or Independent Puritans, who were not separatists'; these New England congregations 'did not at once become separatist, but on the contrary looked upon themselves as true congregations of the Church of England'.[2] John Cotton, in 1648, distinctly claimed that 'the form of Church government wherein we walk doth not differ in substance from that which Mr. Cartwright pleaded'.

England did not allow her emigrants to go to New England without some reluctance. In one sense the discovery of the New World had helped to ease the intolerable problem of religious toleration in Europe. Minorities who were discontented with the situation at home might migrate to territories overseas, in hope of 'God's free air and better things'; the authorities were often glad to let them go, but those who sailed from England were at first carefully supervised, and there was no indiscriminate permission to leave the country. Nevertheless, Puritans in large numbers

[1] A reliable account of all this and of its proud sequel may be found in Dr. C. A. Briggs's *American Presbyterianism* (1885).
[2] Champlin Burrage, *The Early English Dissenters in the Light of Recent Research* (1912), i. 358, 359.

made their way across the Atlantic, including Presbyterian refugees.   Whereas France shut out all foreigners and Huguenots from her North American colonies. When England was parting more or less freely with bold and enterprising lovers of freedom, France under Richelieu's mistaken policy of 1627 was closing the door of Canada to any except Romanists; she would allow no one to enter save orthodox French folk, and at least three ecclesiastics must go to each new settlement.   It proved disastrous in the end for France,[1] but it had the effect of scattering the Huguenot Presbyterians widely among the English both at home and in the transatlantic settlements.   In fact, some reached America by way of Ulster, where they had originally found sanctuary.   The Ulster settlers began to come over during the first half of the eighteenth century in thousands.   Indeed, it was one of these intrepid Ulster Scots, Francis Makemie, who was the pioneer of Presbyterianism in the United States.   He had been educated, like most of the Ulster ministers, at the University of Glasgow.   After some persecution at the hands of the dominant Episcopalians, he succeeded in organizing, about 1705, the first real presbytery in America.   In 1729 the first Synod adopted the Westminster standards. In 1789 the first General Assembly met.   What follows would require a book itself to chronicle, the striking growth of Presbyterian Churches all over the country, and their contribution to the national development. The passion for freedom which is instinctive in the Presbyterian conception of the Church reaches inevitably beyond this region.   In Scotland, as in England, the Presbyterians were thoroughly loyal to monarchy, even

[1] See Francis Parkman's *Pioneers of France*. pp. 441 f.

under sore provocation ; it was not they who swerved
for a time into republicanism.   Indeed, in political life
they are perhaps more often conservative than radical
in their sympathies.   But, in the American situation,
they did not hesitate to show their sympathy with the
cause of political freedom.   It is the American historian
Bancroft who declares that ' the Revolution of 1776,
so far as it was affected by religion, was a Presbyterian
measure.   It was the natural outgrowth of the principles
which the Presbyterianism of the Old World planted
in her sons, the English Puritans, the Scottish Covenanters, the French Huguenots, the Dutch Calvinists,
and the Presbyterians of Ulster '.   When Horace
Walpole satirically complained that Cousin America
had run off with a Presbyterian parson, he was reflecting
the impression made by the rallying of the Presbyterian
settlers to the cause of a free, representative government
in the political no less than in the ecclesiastical sphere
across the Atlantic.   Since then, the various Presbyterian Churches have continued to inspire men for public
service.   No fewer than fifteen Presidents have been
Presbyterians, including recently Cleveland, Roosevelt,
and Woodrow Wilson ; Secretaries of State, leading
citizens, and pioneers in science and industry have also
sprung from these Churches, to represent the public
spirit and mental impetus of their faith.

Alongside of the great Presbyterian Church in the
United States of America there are over half a dozen
Presbyterian Churches, some representing Dutch and
German traditions, others, like the United Presbyterian
Church of North America, the traditions of Scottish
dissent during the eighteenth and nineteenth centuries,
while still others, like the Cumberland Presbyterian

Church, witness to internal divisions of opinion. Super-
ficially it might seem as though the progressives and
the conservatives had been as eager as in Scotland to
witness against each other. But in America the divisions have not been, as in Scotland, over the relation
of the Church to the State ; usually they have split
over doctrinal issues or the effect of revivalism on
Church order, as in English Methodism. They have
been acute, but two factors have helped to mitigate
the evil consequences. One is that owing to the vast
size of the country there has been emulation rather
than overlapping ; the scandalous waste of man-power
and the local friction which Scottish parishes have
endured are much less felt in America. The other
redeeming factor has been the interest in home and
foreign missions. Had the Scottish Churches been
alive to the mission interest, instead of being absorbed
in local strife over scruples, they would have seen and
handled the latter in a more Christian spirit. In
America, while the mission interest has not prevented
schisms in every case, it has worked to heal them.
Petulant divisions would be rendered less likely if
Churches lived up to such a declaration as that of the
Presbyterian Church in the United States of America,
whose General Assembly in 1867 declared that it
regarded ' the whole Church as a missionary society
whose main work is to spread the knowledge of salvation '. Such declarations may be ' words, words,
words '. But this consciousness of the mission purpose
of the Church has meant deeds, from the early days
when Eliot and Brainerd evangelized the native Indian,
to the present age with its far-flung line of missions
stretching from Japan, China, India, and Persia, to

West Africa and South America (Brazil and the Argentine). Their home mission work, particularly in education, is beyond that of any other Presbyterian Church in resourcefulness and organization. Their actual numbers of membership rose from a little over half a million in 1875 to nearly two million in 1925. Indeed, the only country which is any rival to the United States in numerical strength is Holland.

Canada received her Presbyterianism mainly from Scotland. It was ministers from the Scottish Seceders who during the last quarter of the eighteenth century did more than almost anyone else to organize the Church in Nova Scotia, where the Acadians had been succeeded by settlers, many of whom were Presbyterians. After 1825 the aid rendered by the Church of Scotland, in men and money, became increasingly valuable ; the good work advanced, and extended to the Western Provinces. Home divisions were unfortunately transplanted. But the clamant needs and opportunities of the Dominion schooled the Churches into a larger vision, and the year 1875 saw the union of all the Presbyterian Churches in Canada, when the divisions inherited from Scotland were nobly overcome ; mission work at home and abroad went forward, and education was wisely and energetically organized.

The Colonies tell the same kind of tale. It was a Scottish minister who in 1823 gave the first powerful impetus to Presbyterianism in New South Wales, and another Scottish minister was among the pioneers of the strong Presbytery of Melbourne in 1842, which at first was under the Synod of New South Wales. Similarly the Church in New Zealand was inspired and organized by ministers from the Church of Scotland, from 1840 onwards. The effects of the disruption in 1843 were severely felt in these Churches, but union before long was consummated. No more staunch Presbyterian Church was formed than that of Otago, which owed its origin to members of the Free Church of Scotland in 1848, under the lead of the Rev. Thomas Burns, a nephew of the Scottish poet.

The Dutch also carried their Presbyterian Church with them into their colonial empire, once far larger than it is to-day, when it is restricted to Dutch Guiana and the Dutch islands like Java in their East Indian possessions. Elsewhere, as at Ceylon, however, Dutch congregations still survive alongside of the British. By far the most powerful Presbyterian community which owes its origin to the Netherlands is the Dutch Reformed Church of South Africa. It was later, in 1897, that the Presbyterian Church of South Africa, which was recruited mainly from the Scots settlers, became freely organized for its mission to Scots and natives alike.

(b) These movements of expansion were all missions, in one sense. But they were mainly missions to men of the same race. Foreign missions, in the sense of missions to men of all colours and races, started with the Dutch Church in the sixteenth century; it should be remembered that Grotius wrote his *De Veritate Religionis Christianæ* as a text-book for his fellow-countrymen as they might be engaged, in the wake of the Dutch empire overseas, in evangelizing the natives. The Dutch were the first to take seriously the responsibility which their imperial expansion brought in its train, of carrying the Gospel to more than the white settlers. When the East India Company brought

England into the East Indies, the mission activity was much slower to awaken. Indeed, when the Scottish Missionary Society was founded, in 1796, its first spheres were in West Africa and Southern Russia, not in India, where Dr. Alexander Duff founded the first of the great educational colleges in 1829. Since then the work of the Scottish Churches in every sphere of Indian life has been conspicuous and fruitful, going from strength to strength. The Irish Church began to co-operate in 1840. Seven years later the English Church broke ground in China, where W. C. Burns was the pioneer of their mission.

The French Churches started their famous Basuto mission in 1833. But South Africa has owed more to the Scottish Churches; explorers like Mungo Park and Livingstone were Scotsmen who opened up the country for such great missions as those of Lovedale, Livingstonia, Kikuyu, and Nyasaland. The American missions started in 1833 in Africa and India, five years later in China; since then they have spread and are spreading.

This is a bare, brief outline of what has been one of the glories of the Churches during the nineteenth century, their educational, evangelistic, medical, and industrial missions. It takes no account of special missions by several Churches in this immediate environment, nor of missions to Jews and Mahommedans, all of which mark the catholicity of Presbyterianism. But a line or two must be spared for two of the modern developments. One is, the movement in many mission-fields towards the fusion of Presbyterian missions with those of other Churches, in the interests of catholicity and progress. The other, which is allied to it, is the rise of independent native Churches, under the surge of a nascent national consciousness. Neither has been without difficulties of adjustment. But there is no more interesting and healthy example of the latter movement than the Church of Korea or Chosen, which in 1908, within half a century of its planting by foreign missionaries, organized itself as an indigenous Presbyterian Church, with foreign missions of its own. Since 1910 there have been severe political difficulties, but the vigour of this patriotic Church is unimpaired. It is a significant proof that the Presbyterian polity thrives on some foreign soils as a native growth, instead of being merely an importation from Europe.

Such expansion still proceeds. Let this be set down, meantime : at the Alliance of the Reformed Churches holding the Presbyterian System, which held its twelfth General Council at Cardiff in 1925, the total membership was found to have grown by over two millions within twelve years, and the number of adherents was carefully reckoned to be about forty millions.

CHAPTER VII

THE DOCTRINE OF THE CHURCH

ALL this witnesses to two saving notes of the Presbyterian Church, life and catholicity. If there was one truth which the Reformers of the sixteenth century upheld, in regard to Church polity, it was the catholicity of the Church; they disowned any interruption of the historic continuity of the Church. It may be argued, and it is still argued in some quarters, that their theory was better than their practice; but they steadily and conscientiously maintained that in breaking away from the mediæval Roman constitution of Western Catholicism, they were conserving the true catholic, apostolic Church, which was not to be identified with obedience to the Pope of Rome and a hierarchical polity.

In this and the following chapters I think it better to let some of the authoritative or historical statements of the Church speak for themselves. Now, in the original Confession of Faith, as ratified by the Church of Scotland in 1560, it is declared:—

As we believe in one God—Father, Son, and Holy Ghost—so do we most constantly believe that from the beginning there has been, now is, and to the end of the world shall be, one Kirk; that is to say, one company and multitude of men chosen of God, who rightly worship and embrace Him by true faith in Christ Jesus, Who is the only Head of the same Kirk . . . which Kirk is catholick, that is, universal, because it contains the elect of all ages, all realms, nations, and tongues . . . out of the which Kirk there is neither life nor eternal felicity.

The Westminster Confession of Faith is equally outspoken.

The catholick or universal Church, which is invisible, consists of the whole number of the elect that have been, were, or shall be gathered into one, under Christ the Head thereof. . . . The visible Church, which is also catholick or universal under the Gospel (not confined to one nation, as before under the law), consists of all those throughout the world that profess the true religion, together with their children ; and is the kingdom of the Lord Jesus Christ, the house and family of God, out of which there is no ordinary possibility of salvation.

This is the true doctrine of the invisible Church, not as an inward community of the really spiritual which exists side by side with the mixed visible institution of the Church, but as the communion of those who have died, of those who are now alive, and of those yet to be born. The Confession describes the Church in its two aspects, as seen by God alone and as a phenomenon of human experience and observation.

Unto this catholick visible Church Christ hath given the ministry, oracles, and ordinances of God, for the gathering and perfecting of the saints in this life, to the end of the world ; and doth by His own presence and Spirit, according to His promise, make them effectual thereunto.

What this implies may be gathered from some words by Dr. George Hill, who was Principal of St. Mary's College in St. Andrews University from 1791 to 1819. His *View of the Constitution of the Church of Scotland*

(1817) and his famous *Lectures in Divinity* [1] are authoritative and scholarly statements of Presbyterian principles and practice. 'The Christian Church', he declares in the latter treatise (vol. ii, p. 496), 'is to be regarded in a much higher light than as a voluntary association. It is a society created by divine institution.' There may be some who think of the Church as an outward association of pious Christian people, as a more or less secondary and adventitious aid to individual salvation, or as a fabric constructed by citizens of the State for a departmental purpose. Such have not been the thoughts of Presbyterian churchmen. And, lest any should imagine that this is merely an historical relic of the past and not a living tradition, two recent testimonies may be cited. One is from *The Articles of the Faith*, a credal statement approved by the Synod of the Presbyterian Church of England in 1890, where the Seventeenth Article is as follows :—

We acknowledge one holy catholic Church, the innumerable company of saints of every age and nation . . . further, we receive it as the will of Christ that His Church on earth should exist as a visible and sacred brotherhood, consisting of those who profess faith in Jesus Christ and obedience to Him, together with their children . . . and we acknowledge, as a part, more or less pure, of this universal brotherhood, every particular Church throughout the world which professes this faith in Jesus Christ and obedience to Him, as Divine Lord and Saviour.

The *Brief Statement of the Reformed Faith*, published by authority of the General Assembly of the Presbyterian Church in the United States of America (1922) is equally explicit :—

[1] I quote from the third edition, published in 1833.

We believe in the Holy Catholic Church, of which Christ is the only Head. We believe that the Church invisible consists of all the redeemed, and that the Church visible embraces all who profess the true religion, together with their children. We receive to our communion all who confess and obey Christ as their divine Lord and Saviour, and we hold fellowship with all believers in Him.

Instead of saying that there is an invisible Church and a visible Church, we say that the Church is both visible and invisible. This is the Augustinian doctrine which was reproduced in Calvin's view. The Church is invisible in this sense that we do not see it ; we cannot absolutely identify the empirical organization with the real community of those who are truly united to the Body of Christ. In the latter aspect the Church is an object of faith, just as the Holy Spirit is. ' I believe in the Holy Ghost, the Holy Catholic Church.' We believe in it by an act of faith, not because we see its credentials on paper, nor because it appears before us as an external phenomenon of history and social organization. But inasmuch as the faithful gather round the Word and the sacraments, which are visible, and make a more or less creditable and visible profession of faith, this Church is also visible. From the first, the Church has lived and moved in history, as a *cœtus fidelium*, which becomes an institution as it develops the aims and object of its fellowship.

' Unto this catholick visible Church Christ hath given the ministry, oracles, and ordinances of God ', adds the Westminster Confession of Faith (xxv. 3), ' and doth by His own presence and Spirit, according to His promise make them effectual.' The Church consists indeed of

those who ' profess the true religion ', but it is the real
presence of Christ which constitutes the Church, not
mere profession of faith.   Similarly Calvin (*Instit.*, IV.
i. 7–9) points out that ' Church ' sometimes means the
Church as it really is before God, and sometimes the
empirical fellowship of those who profess the Christian
faith, i.e. of baptized persons who ' by partaking of the
Lord's Supper profess unity in true doctrine and charity,
agree in holding the Word of God, and observe the
ministry which Christ has appointed for the preaching
of the Word '.   In this Church, he adds, there is a
large, distressing mixture of hypocrites, of inconsistent
and formal members.   ' *Plurimi sunt fores ovi, plurimi
lupi intus* ', Augustine had said, in protesting that the
visible and the invisible Church were not one and the
same thing ; ' there are many sheep outside the fold,
many wolves within '.   Calvin quotes this with approval.
He points out that the Lord knows them that are His,
the Lord alone ; we cannot have a *certitudo fidei* as to
our neighbour's state before God, and therefore it is
not for us to read his heart and say whether his profession of faith is genuine or false.   God assigns us ' the
judgment of charity, whereby we acknowledge all as
members of the Church who by confession of faith,
regularity of conduct, and participation in the sacraments, unite with us in acknowledging the same God
and Christ '.   This by no means involves any laxity.
The Church has the right to insist on a credible profession
of faith, i.e. on a profession of faith which commends
itself to the charitable but strict judgment of the
Church.   In admitting members, and in admitting them
periodically to the sacraments, the Church has the
right and duty of discipline.   But, as one of the soundest

Presbyterian churchmen declares,[1] 'the Puritan or Independent theory of the Church, that it consists exclusively of those who are deemed regenerate, and their minor children, has unfortunately gained ascendency over many of her ministers and members. . . . This theory is thoroughly opposed to the common faith of the Church, and, as we think, to the plain teachings of the New Testament'. The Presbyterian Church steadily refuses to identify the Church exclusively with true believers or saints, as sects like the Novatians and Donatists of old did, or as Anabaptists and modern sectaries continue to do. And this is where the Presbyterian stress upon discipline and its horror of schism emerge. Both of these principles are vital.

Of discipline and its function in our Churches I have already said something. It survives to-day in a much less thoroughgoing and inquisitive form than under the older ethical conditions of social life. But it is still recognized as a necessary and painful duty, falling to ministers and kirk-sessions, presbyteries, and assemblies upon occasion. Often an offending member may be dealt with privately, after the case has come before the kirk-session. Sometimes, however, the offence may be of so public a nature that the scandal has to be taken up in the public courts of the Church, as when a member is guilty of something that is a reproach to religion, or when a minister falls into grave impropriety of conduct, or when heretical teaching is alleged against a minister or professor of theology. In all cases Christian wisdom is necessary, and in the latter cases

[1] Dr. Charles Hodge of Princeton, in his book on *The Church and its Polity*, pp. 245, 246.

a fair, open trial is secured. The offender, if proved guilty, is either admonished, or, if need be, deposed from office in the congregation or in the Church, or suspended from full communion, or, in rare and extreme cases, solemnly excommunicated. The procedure is carefully guarded, to avoid anything like harshness or respect of persons. Its religious value naturally depends upon the Christian temper in which it is executed, but both at home and in the mission-field it proves a real service to the purity of the Church's fellowship, even in our modern conditions.

The shrinking from schism [1] is not less characteristic. The 'truth of the unity of the Catholik visible Church is the main ground of all Church union and communion', says Durham in his seventeenth-century *Treatise Concerning Scandal* (part iv, ch. 1), one of the most searching and wise books upon the ethical practice of the Church and Christians. He discusses frankly the various causes of schisms and divisions, but refuses to admit that any failings in the Church ever justify separation. The Church may make a mistake in failing to censure an unworthy minister or member; it may admit some who are unworthy; and so on. 'These indeed are faults, but they are not such as make a Church to be no Church; and tho' these have sometimes been pretended to be the causes of schisms and divisions in the Church in practice, yet were they never defended to be just grounds of schisms and divisions, but were ever condemned by all councils and fathers, and cannot be in reason sustained' (ch. 7). Look at

---

[1] I had made this little catena before I came across Dr. G. W. Sprott's strong pamphlet on *The Doctrine of Schism in the Church of Scotland* (1902).

the torn, unsatisfactory state of the Corinthian Church as depicted in St. Paul's Epistles to the Corinthians, he adds :—

> Many things of that kind were defective in the Church of Corinth, where the Sacrament was so disorderly administrated, confusion in many things of worship, and some things still to be set in order ; yet doth the apostle nowhere press union more than in these epistles. . . . If there be defects of that kind, it is union and not division that is to be looked upon as the commended mean for redressing of the same.

Durham is thoroughly representative of Presbyterianism when he repudiates schism and division as being worse evils than the evils they profess to avoid. Calvin had urged that to withdraw from the Church was to renounce the Lord, to deny God and Christ. If a Church possessed the Word and the sacraments, then no amount of error or shortening in minor matters could ever justify Christians in withdrawing from it. He and the other Reformers left the Church of Rome, not for the mere reason that it had become morally inferior, but because it had ceased to be a Church by its perversion of sound doctrine and its abuse of the Christian sacraments. And they continued to maintain that no amount of dissatisfaction with the visible Church, on the score of inconsistent life and practice, gave any Christian the right to secede.

We have already stated [he writes in the *Institutio Christianæ Religionis* (IV. ii. 1)] the importance attached by us to the ministry of the Word and the sacraments, and the extent of our reverence for it, that it may be accounted by us as a sure token for distinguishing the Church. That is to say, wherever this exists entire and unspoiled (*integrum et illibatum*), no faults or diseases of

H

conduct prevent us from maintaining the name of
" Church ".

This is the invariable line taken by Presbyterian
churchmen like Durham, who saw the principles of
their faith. They started back in horror from schism.
' Schism ', says Durham, ' is one of the greatest hurts
that can come to an orthodox Church, it being next
to heresy in doctrine ; and therefore no particular evil
can be laid in the balance with it.' Durham as minister
of Glasgow Cathedral under the Commonwealth had
to warn his people against the Cromwellian sectaries.
The factious spirit was already invading the Church
when he lived ; fortunately he died, at the early age
of thirty-six, before the root of bitterness in jarring
quarrels between his fellow-churchmen had endangered
Christian unity.

Even in sixteenth-century England so intransigeant
a reformer as Cartwright annoyed the extremist Puritans
by refusing to secede from the Church on account of
ceremonial rites and vestments. Like the others, he
regarded the surplice and the use of the cross in baptism
as ' dregs of Popery ' ; but this narrow view did not
shut him up to the course of advocating withdrawal
from the Church on the score of such practices. He
agreed with the Puritan Presbyterians to whom the
idea of schism or separation was abhorrent. ' As for
separation from a worship for some errors of a Church,
the independency of single congregations, a Church of
visible saints, and other tenets of Brownists, they are
contrary to God's Word.' So Samuel Rutherford in
one of his letters. In these very days, when the duty
of Church discipline was being urged, and anything
like Latitudinarian principles denounced with vigour,

man like George Gillespie could appeal to his fellow-Christians in England :—

Oh, brethren, we shall be one in heaven; let us pack up our differences in this place of our pilgrimage the best way we can. . . . How much better is it that you be one with the other Reformed Churches, though somewhat straitened and bound up, than to be divided, though at full liberty and elbow-room! " Better is a dry morsel, and quietness therewith, than a house full of sacrifices with strife."

The Second Helvetic Confession, recognized and approved by the Church of Scotland, had already taught Christians to mark carefully

wherein the truth and unity of the Church consists, lest we either rashly breed or nourish schisms in the Church. It consists not in outward rites and ceremonies, but rather in the truth and unity of the catholic faith. This catholic faith is not taught us by the ordinances or laws of men [the Council of Trent, be it remembered, was in session when this was composed], but by the holy Scriptures, a compendious and short sum whereof is the Apostles' Creed.

For many reasons it is timely to recall and underline this. 'The doctrine of our Presbyterianism in the day of its power and glory', says Dr. James Walker in his classical monograph upon *Scottish Theology and Theologians* (second edition, 1888, pp. 103 f.), was 'a very high doctrine of the catholic visible Church. Schism was a great reality'. And even when the apple of discord fell among the Scottish Presbyterians, even when their divisions rendered Church unity a matter of religious idealism rather than an actuality of fellowship in the country, the sense and need of an undivided Church did not lose hold of the Scottish mind. One instance may be cited. At the Revolution settlement in 1690, the three ministers of the extremist Covenanting party joined the Church of Scotland, simply because, though dissatisfied with the Church's wise refusal to make the Covenants obligatory, they were not satisfied that any scruples about fellowship with less rigid Christians would justify them in keeping outside the Church. Unfortunately, some of their people failed to follow this good lead, and perpetuated a denomination. But Alexander Shields, one of these three ministers, declared frankly that while there might be conceivably good grounds for a conscientious secession, yet 'endeavours for union and concord among the lovers of truth are duties absolutely necessary'. So poignantly did this Cameronian minister feel the sin of schism. He was true to the Presbyterian conception of the Church, as something more than a body of those who share the same opinions or as a society to which one need only belong if one is sure of getting all one likes within it.

Switzerland, Holland, America, and Scotland have all contributed records of internal dissensions which denote a failure to realize the essential catholicity of the Church, and the corresponding guilt of schism. St. Peter in his first Epistle warns his fellow-presbyters against behaving like 'lords over God's heritage', or, as Tyndale's version had it, 'as though ye were lordes over the parishes'. It was a prophetic warning, which has been repeatedly required in the history of the Church. Schisms and separations imply guilt on both sides, though the proportion varies. There may be, as there has often been, in those who break away, a spirit of levity and perversity, self-will disguised as zeal, an exaggerated sense of what is due to scruples,

an infatuation with prejudices which have been baptized
as principles, or some petulant, local temper which
loves to dwell on differences rather than on affinities.
Censoriousness and spiritual pride have too often worked
in the minorities who seceded.   But on the other hand,
there has been the guilt of overbearing conduct in the
majority.   Round every Presbyterian Church, sometimes within its polity and sometimes as sectarian
congregations, there are groups of Christians who might
have been retained within the unity of the Church,
had the leaders of the majority exercised more tact and
consideration.   But when they have preferred to drive
rather than to lead, or to use their majority even to
carry out a legitimate enterprise, without Christian
respect to the rank and file, when presbyters either
individually or collectively have pressed their authority,
as was the case in the Church of Scotland in 1752, for
example, the result has too frequently been a split,
which is long of healing.   The Presbyterian Churches,
just because they are Churches, and just because they
are not clerical, are in special danger of this.   It is one
temptation of their organized strength, and they have
occasionally tended to be tyrannous in the exercise of
that strength, especially in dealing with those who are
opinionative and annoying.   I imagine that what
makes some pleas for Christian unity ineffective among
us is that people have the fixed impression that they
are being put forward by those who seem to dislike any
opposition to the mechanical rule of a majority.

Our record is not good.   In almost every country it
is the same tale : divided Churches, and reunions
difficult.   Presbyterian Churches are specially liable to
sharp dissensions, through their very freedom of dis-

cussion, and their keen, diffused interest in theology. They may plead, not altogether unjustly, that unity is not the same thing as uniformity, that Churches may agree to differ, and so on. Yet their own doctrine of the Church is not to be evaded. It is all very well to say that ' schism ' is a misleading metaphor ; inorganic substances like cloth can be rent, and the result is loss, but in the organic world scission or schism is a means of perpetuating life, and therefore the existence of different Churches in the Christian sphere may be justified ; they may be a proof of intensive vitality in the organism. On paper this is logical. But in actual practice, while it would be absurd to contend that separation from the visible polity of the Church is never a duty, the lamentable fact remains, plain as a steeple on the landscape, that separations have often been due to wilfulness and have been almost inevitably accompanied by censoriousness and bitter feeling. Worldliness is a besetting sin of large Churches, and no serious Christian would for an instant seek to palliate it. But small Churches and sects, in their recoil from it, slip easily into spiritual pride, and the Lord Jesus regarded censoriousness or uncharitable temper as the most heinous sin among His followers. When it stiffens into a refusal to admit other Christians to the Lord's Table, it becomes unspeakably sinful. And this, we must confess, has happened in our Scottish Presbyterianism. ' An old Highlander, when his minister was speaking to him about the Church, exclaimed, " *Eaglais ! chan'eil ach bleighdean de dh'Eaglais againn* " (Church ! we have only splinters of a Church). The significance of the old man's exclamation will be appreciated when we consider that, in a sparsely popu-

lated parish, he had before his eyes the sad spectacle
of four different Presbyterian Churches, whose members
could not unite in partaking together of what each
believed to be the great Sacrament of Christian fellowship.' [1] This is worse even than the case of those
denominations which shut out from the Communion
Table all save those who have been either immersed
or episcopally confirmed, worse because these Presbyterian Churches have the same creed and polity. It
would be healing and hopeful if some recovery of our
true doctrine about the Church brought us to the point
reached by our American brethren in the year 1758,
when the sharply divided Synods of New York and
Philadelphia declared that they were deeply conscious
that 'the present divided state of the Presbyterian
Church in this land . . . tends to weaken its interests,
to dishonour religion, and consequently its glorious
Author', and earnestly counselled all under their care
that 'instead of indulging a contentious disposition,
they would love each other with a pure heart, fervently,
as brethren who profess subjection to the same Lord,
adhere to the same faith, worship, and government,
and entertain the same hope of glory'.

Even short of mutual excommunication, secessions
are apt to generate a heat of spiritual pride which is
the shadow cast by zeal. Thus in the Free Church of
Scotland, after 1843, this was not only deplored by
some of its truest members as well as denounced by
its opponents, but regretted by sympathetic critics in
other Churches, as, for example, by the saintly Thomas
Erskine of Linlathen. 'I doubt not', he wrote on

[1] *The Celtic Church and the See of St. Peter*, by J. C. McNaught,
B.D. (1927), p. 111.

June 7, 1843, 'that a certain kind and degree of good may arise amongst certain persons out of our Scotch Kirk separation—more awakened thought, more zeal— but I fear also more judging, more spiritual pride, as in the much and perhaps overlauded days of the Covenant and the hillside.' The courage and idealism and self-sacrifice which inspired the churchmen of Scotland, even in their fallings out with one another, are a source of legitimate pride and a moral inspiration to those who care for the spiritual independence of the Church of Christ. But secessions, however high-minded, have their risks, and it is no disloyalty to the past to admit that these risks were not always avoided. It was a resolute Free Churchman, the late Principal Rainy, who in 1887 told the General Assembly of his own Church that they had been guilty sometimes of making God's goodness to them as a Church the occasion of pride. 'At the Disruption, and in the days that followed, we had ground for the most copious and emphatic thanksgiving. We were as men that dreamed ; the Lord had done great things for us. Did we escape the temptation to turn this goodness into an occasion for arrogance and scorn ? Looking back, I say no. We did not escape it. Therein we sinned.'

It is painful and humiliating to recall such faults and defects among good men. But my point is, that where they have abounded, to the scandal of Christen-dom, it has been due to a defective Presbyterianism ; such reproaches to the Gospel are at bottom the result of a failure to recognize and to realize the true meaning of the Church as taught by Presbyterianism at its best, in its essential catholicity.

CHAPTER VIII

THE MINISTRY AND THE SACRAMENTS

I

'THE members of the Church of Rome and of the Episcopal and Presbyterian Churches agree', says Principal Hill, 'in opposing the presumptuous conclusion, by which a spirit of fanaticism would represent the offices of a standing ministry as useless.'[1] The positive conclusion is, as has been already outlined, a ministry of the Church in the discharge of the various functions originally assigned to presbyters in the apostolic Church.

' Presbyters '—for, while all Christians are priests to God, none is priest, in any official sense, to others. The Presbyterian Churches do not use the term ' priest ' at all for their ministers. Hooker saw no great difficulty in using the term metaphorically for the ministry, on the ground that, as the Church had ' properly now no sacrifice ' in the Communion, so the name of ' priesthood ' no more drew the minds of people ' to any cogitation of sacrifice than the name of a senator or of an alderman causeth them to think upon old age '. But this is a real source of misconception. Since Hooker did not feel it to be so, he could freely admit that it was all one, whether we spoke of priesthood, or presbytership, or ministry ; indeed, he preferred

[1] *Lectures in Divinity*, ii. 431.

'presbyter', a word which, as he admits, 'doth seem more fit, and in propriety of speech more agreeable than priest with the drift of the whole Gospel of Jesus Christ'. 'The Holy Ghost throughout the body of the New Testament making so much mention of them doth not anywhere call them priests.'[1] Yet 'minister is a better name for the clergy. It has not been soiled, as 'pastor' has been for many of us, by smug, sanctimonious associations, and it is free from the sacerdotal misconceptions which attach to 'priest'. Ruskin was right in his *Notes on the Construction of Sheepfolds* (15), when he pointed out: 'As for the unhappy retention of the term Priest in our English Prayer Book, so long as it was understood to mean nothing but an upper order of Church officer . . . there was little harm in it ; but, now that this order of clergy begins to presume upon a title which, if it mean anything at all, is simply short for Presbyter, and has no more to do with Hiereus than with the term Levite, it is time that some order should be taken both with the book and the clergy.' That is no concern of Presbyterian churchmen. Their sole concern is to make it clear that, in adhering to the term Presbyter, they are true to the practice of the apostolic Church, in word and in spirit ; as they ignore Priest and employ Presbyter, they are doing something far more important than maintaining an archaic title for their ministers.

The Church exists to serve and to be served, not to govern and be governed. The primary question about the Church is not its form of polity but its function in the saving order of God, and questions of government only arise in this connexion. Yet the very term

[1] *Ecclesiastical Polity*, V, lxxviii. 2, 3.

'ministry' indicates that the service and the government of the Church are vitally connected. In one sense
all faithful members of the Church are ministers; each
can and ought to render some service to the cause of
Christ. But a Church involves special services, so
responsible and exacting, that they are delegated to a
certain number, who are called ministers. The ministry
is therefore more than a number of Christians set apart
to act for the collective body of the faithful, as its
representatives and agents. It is a vocation from Christ
Himself. Presbyters receive their ministry from the
Lord; they serve the Church, it is true—it would be
more true to say that they serve in the Church, or in
the special congregation to which they are called; but
One is their Master, and they serve Him, as apostles
and ambassadors of the Gospel.

How deeply the Church of Scotland regarded this
apostolic ministry of presbyters may be gathered from
its *Sum of Saving Knowledge* (the seventeenth-century
work of Durham and Gillespie), where it is explained
that in 2 Corinthians v. 19–20,

the apostle teacheth us . . . that albeit the hearing,
believing, and obeying of this word [of reconciliation to
God] doth belong to all those to whom this Gospel doth
come, yet the office of preaching of it with authority
belongeth to none, but to such only as God doth call to
His ministry, and sendeth out with commission for this
work. This the apostle holdeth forth in these words,
'We are ambassadors for Christ, as though God did
beseech you by us'.

Also,

that the ministers of the Gospel should behave themselves
as Christ's messengers, and should closely follow their

commission set down in His Word (Matthew xxviii. 19, 20) ; and when they do so, they should be received by the people as ambassadors from God, for here the apostle in all their names saith, ' We are ambassadors for Christ, as though God did beseech **you** by us.'

No words could state more plainly the seriousness and responsibility of the ministry for ministers themselves, as well as the obligation to listen to the Gospel thus faithfully proclaimed. Both rest upon the conviction that the ministry is fully apostolic, and that while office and order in the Church are not external bonds imposed upon the community of the faithful, yet neither are they merely the expression by the community of its need for unity and authority, as though ministers simply were a convenient representation of the corporate consciousness of the Church. They fulfil the functions of the apostles, who were sent by Christ or given by Christ Himself to the Church. In the antithesis used by the authors of the *Jus Divinum*, ' ministers are sent to the people, not by the people '.

This raises the whole question of ordination, and the mind of the Church upon ordination is explicit. In the *Form of Presbyterial Church Government*, which was approved by the General Assembly of the Scottish Church in 1645, the principles are laid down on which all subsequent practice has been based, viz. that a minister must be lawfully called ; ' no man is to be ordained a minister for a particular congregation, if they of that congregation can show just cause of exception against him ', but ' every minister of the Word is to be ordained by imposition of hands, and prayer, with fasting, by those preaching presbyters to whom it doth belong '. ' Ordination is the act of a presbytery'; it is 'the solemn setting apart of a person to some public Church office'. In consonance with this, no one, it is held, can undertake the work of the Christian ministry unless he be lawfully called to it. This lawful call involves a sense, on the part of the individual, of his vocation to be a minister of God; he comes forward to ordination as he is humbly conscious of an inward call from the Lord. But this vocation required to be duly sanctioned by the Church, and this is done in two ways: he is examined as to his qualifications for teaching and preaching the Word of God, and also he must receive a hearty call from some congregation which is desirous and willing to have his services as their minister. The latter is a valuable testimony, corroborating his inward call, but it is not the essence of ordination. 'The function of the people is not to confer the office, but to join in the exercise of a judgment whether a given person is called of God to be a minister, and to decide whether he shall exercise his office over them, as their spiritual guide.' [1] The Church, acting by the presbyters, solemnly attests this judgment, after having been satisfied that the man's qualifications are adequate. And thus the inward call or endowment of the Spirit is duly and regularly recognized, as constituting a ministerial vocation.

In the Church of Scotland the third and the fifth of the solemn questions put to a minister before he is ordained or admitted to a pastoral charge are these:—

Do you acknowledge Presbyterian Church government, as now settled by law, to be the only government of this

---

[1] Dr. C. Hodge, *The Church and its Polity*, p. 143.

Church ; and do you promise to submit thereto, concur therewith, and never endeavour, directly or indirectly, the prejudice or subversion thereof ?

Are not zeal for the honour of God, love to Jesus Christ, and desire of saving souls, your great motives and chief inducements to enter into the functions of the holy ministry, and not worldly designs and interests ?

Before an elder is ordained or admitted, he is asked the following question :—

Do you believe the fundamental doctrines of the Christian faith contained in the Confession of Faith of this Church, and do you approve of the worship, discipline, and government of this Church, and promise never, directly or indirectly, to attempt the prejudice or subversion thereof ?

At the ordination or induction of a minister in the United Free Church of Scotland, the two corresponding questions are these :—

Do you acknowledge the Presbyterian government and discipline, as authorized in this Church, to be founded on, and agreeable to, the Word of God ; do you promise to maintain and submit to the said government and discipline ; and while cherishing a spirit of brotherhood towards all the faithful followers of Christ, do you engage to seek the purity, edification, peace, and extension of this Church ?

Are not zeal for the glory of God, love to the Lord Jesus Christ, and desire of saving souls, and not worldly designs or interests, so far as you know your own heart, your great motives and chief inducements to enter into the office of the holy ministry ?

The former of these questions is also put to elders at their ordination or induction, and the second is put in the following form :—

Are not zeal for the glory of God, and a desire to serve the Lord Jesus Christ, in the work of His kingdom, so

far as you know your own heart, your great motives to
enter into the office of ruling elder ?

Carelessness and faults in regularly appointed ministers
have sometimes provoked people to revert to a state
of Christian fellowship in which such a call and ordination
means nothing ; an individual's gifts are held to justify
him in assuming the ministry, and a congregation elects
him as a constituency elects a member of Parliament
or as a club may select a chairman. But ' We Presbyterians join with the Church of Rome and the Church of
England in holding that the persons vested with Church
government derive their powers, not from the people
but from Jesus Christ by His ministers.' [1] These are
emphatic and authoritative words ; they involve a deep
view of ordination, which, ' considered as the act of
Jesus Christ, by His office-bearers constituting a minister
of the Church universal ', is to be distinguished from
the popular election of the minister by a congregation,
' which is the appointment of men applying or limiting
the exercise of ' the ministerial commission ' in such
manner as they please, and with more or less wisdom,
as it happens '.[2]

Ordination is an act of the presbytery, but in its
specific action it is reserved for presbyters who lay
hands on the person to be ordained, with prayer. ' If
ordination were merely induction into the order of
presbyters, from which some members by a subsequent
process were selected to preach, and others to rule,
then the service might from its nature belong to all
presbyters.' [3] But as ordination to the ministry is the

[1] Principal Hill, *Lectures in Divinity*, ii. 442.
[2] *Ibid.*, ii. 440, 441.
[3] Dr. C. Hodge, *The Church and its Polity*, p. 291.

solemn consecration of a man to the office of presbyter, it is a function which belongs to presbyters as such. The matter has been frequently debated, both in this country and in America, but such is the general decision of the Church. 'No case of lay ordination, or of an ordination in which lay-ruling elders participated, has been produced, or, as is believed, can be produced in the history of any Presbyterian Church'. [1] Logically, it might be argued, ruling elders ought not therefore to vote in a trial for heresy ; but in this case the offence is one that concerns the whole Church, and consequently just as ruling elders are part of the presbytery which ordains, though they do not take part in the laying on of hands, so they participate in the deposition of a minister, although there again the actual sentence is pronounced by the presiding presbyter.

Since ordination is admission to the sacred office of presbyter, it follows that when any elder becomes a minister or presbyter, he has to be re-ordained. The Church defines specifically the duties of the presbyter, and although an elder, or indeed any layman who is specially endowed with the gift, may on occasion teach and preach, yet the regular ministry of the Word and of the Sacraments is reserved by the Church for its ordained presbyters. Even a licentiate, i.e. a student who has been set apart by the presbytery, may not celebrate the Sacraments, although he may preach.

In ordaining, the Church acts by its presbyters as the catholic Church ; the minister is ordained as a presbyter of the whole Church. He is indeed inducted to a special congregation, or, in the case of foreign missions, to a special sphere, but he is to serve the

[1] *Op. cit.*, p. 294.

Church there. A truly ordained person, therefore, cannot be re-ordained. When he is removed to another sphere, he is inducted, but his original ordination remains valid. ' In the same manner as everyone who is baptized becomes a member of the catholic Church, so everyone who is ordained, by the laying on of the hands of the office-bearers of the Church, becomes a minister of the Church universal.' His induction to a special charge ' serves no other purpose than to specify the bounds in which the Church universal, by the hands of whose ministers he received the power, require that the powers shall be exercised '.[1]

All this is based on the rule of the Church, in accordance with the ancient catholic practice, that ordination must be accompanied by induction into a ministerial charge. This is where the right of popular election becomes so vital, for the fact that a minister has been chosen by the people over whom he is to preside invests their relationship with a special spirit of fellowship, and one of the surest tests that his call to the ministry is valid is to be found in the decision of the congregation that he has commended his gifts to them.

Here is one illustration of how profoundly this pastoral tie is valued. Before a congregation proceeds to the arrangements for filling up a vacancy in the pastorate, the Church of Scotland has the following words read to them in the formal intimation :—

The General Assembly, considering how deeply important it is that the steps which are taken for the election of a Minister should be proceeded in with a due sense of the momentous nature of the duty, and an earnest desire and endeavour to discharge it aright, deem it fitting to address

---

[1] Principal Hill, *Lectures in Divinity*, ii. 439.

I

to you some words of counsel. You are now called, as a congregation, to exercise the privileges which belong to you in relation to the appointment of a Minister to this parish. It is impossible to over-estimate the importance of that duty. In making choice of one who is to be your future religious teacher and spiritual guide, you perform an act, the issues of which must be of the most vital moment to yourselves and to the interests of this parish. The welfare of the congregation, the promotion of the cause and kingdom of Christ in this place, and the attainment of the many and great benefits which arise from a successful ministry, depend on your exercising your choice wisely and rightly. Considering, therefore, how solemn the duty is to which you are called, and how serious its consequences will be, let it be your earnest desire and effort to discharge it with thoughtful care. Let it be your aim, and your only aim, in the decisions which you form, to do what you sincerely consider will be most for the good of the Church of Christ. As becomes a Christian congregation, knit together by the common bond of allegiance to Christ, ' let all your things be done with charity ', maintaining towards each other, whatever may be your individual opinions, a spirit of forbearance and peace. Pray also to Almighty God, earnestly beseeching Him to guide you by the grace of His Spirit, so that the various steps which are taken for the election of a Minister to this parish may issue in an appointment which shall be for His glory and for the good of the Church.

Such is the normal attitude of the Church. There may be, of course, exceptional cases in which a Christian undertakes ministerial work upon his own initiative ; Presbyterians have allowed freely that a ministry may originate without formal ordination, as for example in a community where there are none to ordain. ' There may be ', says George Gillespie, ' an extraordinary calling from God where religion is not yet planted, nor Churches yet constituted ; it is altogether another case in a constituted reformed or reforming Church. I add, with Peter Martyr, that even those persons who set about the work of the ministry extraordinarily, or among infidels, if they can come at any who may ordain them in the usual and right way, they ought not to neglect the seeking of ordination.' These last words indicate how earnestly the leaders of the Scottish Church felt the need and duty of ordination to the ministry.

Recognizing that presbyters were admitted to the ministry in the early Church by the laying on of hands, Calvin declared that ' although there is no fixed precept concerning this, yet as we see that it was uniformly observed by the apostles, this careful observance of it by them ought to be equivalent to a precept for us. And certainly it is useful to have the dignity of the ministry commended to the people by such a symbol, and also to have the ordained man reminded that he is no longer his own but bound over in service to God and the Church ' (*Instit.*, IV. iii. 16). Besides, he adds (to quote from the French edition of 1541), the rite will not be an empty sign if it be restored to its original meaning, whereby ' *il est offert et dédié à Dieu pour le servir en cest estat, et que l'Eglise soit incitée a le recommander à Dieu par prières communes* '. The laying on of hands is thus the evidence given of an appointment made and a commission transmitted, the solemn, external expression of a spiritual action on the part of the ordaining presbyters. The essential element is not, of course, contact, but the prayer and blessing thereby symbolized. As the Bishop of Gloucester puts it,[1] ' We ordain with the laying on of

[1] *The Lambeth Joint Report on Church Unity*, p. 139.

hands; and we mean by that, not only that we give
a solemn commission, but that we all unite in prayer
to God. The ordination with laying on of hands is
but a symbolic prayer. The essence of the ordination
lies in the prayer.' As such, it has been constantly
practised in the Scottish Church, except apparently for
a few years after 1560. 'It is undoubtedly true that
the first generation of Reformed preachers had been
nearly all Roman presbyters; that within a few years
they began to ordain new presbyters by the laying on
of hands; and that there is therefore in the Scottish
Presbyterian Churches a *perpetua successio presbyterorum*
from before the Reformation'. [1]

II

According to the *Confession of Faith*, the term
sacrament' is confined to the two rites of Baptism
and the Lord's Supper, 'neither of which may be
dispensed by any but by a minister of the Word, lawfully ordained' (xxvii. 4).

The sacraments are means of grace. 'We utterly
damne the vanitie of those that affirme Sacraments to
be nothing else but naked and bare signs '—so vigorously
do the authors of the Scottish Confession (xxi) speak of
those who misrepresented their sacramental doctrine
(and, lest they misrepresent themselves, 'damne'
means no more than 'condemn').

Whosoever slanders us, as that we affirme and believe
Sacraments to be naked and bare signs, do injurie to us
and speak against the manifest truth.

---

[1] Lord Balfour of Burleigh, *Presbyterianism in Scotland*, p. 44.

The sacraments are 'effectual means of salvation'. In the Shorter Catechism (xcii) a sacrament is defined as 'an holy ordinance instituted by Christ; wherein, by sensible signs [i.e. the water in Baptism, and the bread and wine in Holy Communion] Christ and the benefits of the new covenant are represented, sealed, and applied to believers'. Each of these three terms is significant. 'The spiritual part of both "Sacraments" is Christ and His benefits' (Larger Catechism, clxxvi). This is presented in the Word of God (for Bible-reading truly regarded is sacramental), and represented or set forth over again in the 'sensible signs' of the sacraments, which are not mere signs or symbols. 'I call them not signs', said Robert Bruce, the great Edinburgh minister of the sixteenth century, 'I call them not signs because they represent only, but I call them signs because they have the body and blood of Christ conjoined with them . . . because God has made them potent instruments to deliver that same thing which they signify.' The sacraments 'seal' or ratify Christ as the Life and Soul of the rite to the participant; they also 'apply' Christ and His benefits, actually imparting and conveying grace. And this is for 'believers'; the sacraments are for receptive faith, they 'become effectual means of salvation, not from any virtue in them, or in him that doth administer them, but only by the blessing of Christ and the working of His Spirit in them that by faith receive them' (Shorter Catechism, xci). Sacraments in the Church are a badge and a bond of loyalty, but only as they are a direct participation in the living Christ. They are, as the *Confession of Faith* sums it up (xxvii. 1), holy signs and seals of the covenant of grace, immediately instituted by God, to represent Christ and His benefits, and to confirm our interest in Him ; as also to put a visible difference between those that belong to the Church and the rest of the world ; and solemnly to engage them to the service of God in Christ, according to His Word.

The function of the sacraments is therefore primarily to quicken and sustain the communion of the Christian with the living Lord, and thereby to deepen the unworldliness of the Church, i.e. the sense that the Church lives by powers drawn from deeper sources than the State or the social order, and also to inspire the sense of dutiful service of God, ' service ' meaning worship in its widest implications.

(*a*) Baptism is more than a formal ceremony of initiation or admission into the Church ; it is a sacrament of regeneration.

Baptism is a sacrament of the New Testament, ordained by Jesus Christ, not only for the solemn admission of the party baptized into the visible Church, but also to be unto him a sign and seal of the covenant of grace, of his ingrafting into Christ, of regeneration, of remission of sins, and of his giving up unto God through Jesus Christ, to walk in newness of life (*Confession of Faith*, xxviii. 1).

The Presbyterian Church, it is almost needless to say, maintained the continuity of catholic practice by baptizing the infant children of Church members ; it was never Baptist. ' Not only those that do actually profess faith in and obedience unto Christ, but also the infants of one or both believing parents are to be baptized' (*Confession of Faith*, xxviii. 4). In the *Directory* it is laid down that ' the child to be baptized, after notice given to the minister the day before, is to be presented by the father, or (in case of his necessary absence) by some Christian friend in his place '. Indeed, by an Act of the 1917 General Assembly of the Church of Scotland, it is enacted that

a child has a right to baptism whose parents, one or both, having been themselves baptized, profess the Christian religion and desire baptism for the child ; or who, being of unknown parentage or otherwise separated from its parents, is under Christian care and guardianship. But inasmuch as it is the practice of the Church to demand sponsors at the dedication of children to God in baptism, who shall covenant for their education in the faith of Christ, ministers are enjoined to have regard to this requirement in the light of the Act, 1712.

This 1712 Act provided that a kirk-session might act as sponsors, in the case of foundling children, and that sponsors, relatives if possible, must present the child, ' if parents be dead, or absent, or grossly ignorant, or under scandal, or contumacious '.

The *Confession of Faith* explains (xxviii. 6) that ' the efficacy of baptism is not tied to that moment of time wherein it is administered ', any more than the efficacy of the Communion is tied ; they reach deeper than the consciousness of the Christian at the moment. ' Yet, notwithstanding ', the Confession continues, in order to prevent the idea that the rite is formal, ' by the right use of this ordinance the grace promised is not only offered but really exhibited and conferred by the Holy Ghost to such (whether of age or infants) as that grace belongeth unto, according to the counsel of God's own will, in His appointed time.'

The sacrament of Baptism, according to the *Directory*, was to be administered by a minister of Christ only, 'not in any case by any private person', and never to be celebrated 'in private places or privately but in the place of public worship and in face of the congregation'.

So with marriage. 'The minister . . . is publickly to solemnize it in the place appointed by authority for publick worship, before a competent number of credible witnesses, at some convenient hour of the day, at any time of the year, except on a day of publick humiliation. And we advise that it be not upon the Lord's day'. Marriages had been commonly celebrated on Sunday in Scotland, but this had led to some undesirable and irreverent junketing. Hence the new regulation.

Unlike the sacrament of Holy Communion, baptism 'is but once to be administered to any person'. There are few explicit directions about the rite, except that 'the party is to be baptized in the name of the Father, and of the Son, and of the Holy Ghost, by a minister of the Gospel, lawfully called thereunto' (*Confession of Faith*, xxviii. 2), and that 'the outward element to be used in this sacrament is water' (i.e. the mediæval additions of unction, etc., were excluded). The method is not rigidly fixed; 'dipping of the person into the water is not necessary, but baptism is rightly administered by pouring or sprinkling water upon the person' (*Confession of Faith*, xxviii. 3).

Calvin wished to revise and retain the rite of Confirmation, as in the early Church, i.e. a service in which a boy of ten would present himself to the Church and be catechized upon his belief. 'Thus, while the whole Church looked on, and witnessed, he would profess the one true sincere faith with which the body of the faithful, in common consent, worship the one God.' He thought a special catechism should be drawn up, for such questions and answers; furthermore, he wished to see ministers still laying hands on the catechumen by way of blessing, to lend reverence and dignity to the sacred service. 'This laying on of hands, which is done simply by way of a blessing, I commend, and would like to see restored to its pure use at the present day' (*Instit.*, IV. xix. 4–13). The Scottish Commissioners failed to persuade the Westminster Assembly to agree to some recognition of a similar rite for the solemn admission of catechumens to the Lord's Table. But in practice this is done. The young people are specially trained in a class by the minister, dealt with privately upon the question of personal religion, and admitted by the minister and kirk-session, with the right hand of fellowship, in presence of the congregation. The American Church directs the minister ' to lay his hand, if such be his discretion, upon the head of everyone in order, kneeling before him '. It might be well if this custom were followed, though it cannot claim catholic precedent.

(*b*) We confess and undoubtedly believe that the faithful, in the right use of the Lord's Table, do so eat the body and drink the blood of the Lord Jesus, that he remains in them and they in him : yea, that they are so made flesh of his flesh and bone of his bones, that as the Eternal Godhead hath given to the flesh of Christ Jesus (which of the own condition and nature was mortal and corruptible) life and immortality, so doth Christ Jesus' flesh and blood, eaten and drunken by us, give to us the same prerogatives. . . . We affirm that the faithful, in the right use of the Lord's Table, have such conjunction [union] with Christ Jesus as the natural man cannot comprehend : yea and further we affirm that albeit the faithful, oppressed by negligence and manlie [human] infirmity, do not profit so much as they would at the very instant action of the

Supper, yet it shall after bring forth fruit as lively [living] seed sown in good ground ; for the Holy Spirit, which can never be divided from the right institution of the Lord Jesus, will not frustrate the faithful of the fruit of that mystical action.

So the original *Confession of Faith* (xxi) of 1560. It is needless, especially after what has been already said, to add anything by way of exposition to this massive statement. But one or two details may be supplied, to illustrate the practice of the Churches.

The book-boards in the church-pews and the Communion Table are covered with fair, white cloth ; the elders reverently carry the bread and wine into church and lay them on the Communion Table, behind which stands the minister. After the prayer of consecration, he hands them to the elders, who distribute them to the people. They receive the elements, passing them from one to the other, as a symbol of Christian fellowship, after the manner of the first Lord's Supper. This differs from the practice of members coming up individually to receive the elements. It was introduced by Zwingli at Zurich, who asks the King of France : ' Let not your Majesty be offended at this custom of receiving and giving ; for it has been often found that some who happened to sit together, but who had formerly had feuds and mutual hatred, have laid aside the passion of their minds as they partook together of the bread or of the cup.'

It is the rule of the Church that the Sacrament be always accompanied by the Word, to prevent any superstitious abuse ; the Sacrament is the vivid expression of what the Word contains, i.e. the living presence of the Lord, and therefore, to partake of it with intelligent devotion, the Word is to be preached before the Sacrament. In olden days this sermon was called ' the Action Sermon ', a phrase which came from the Latin phrase *actio gratiarum*, recalling, as the term ' Eucharist ' does in another way, the glad thankfulness which is intended to pervade the service.

In this service Presbyterian worship reaches its height of reverence and austere impressiveness. The minister, in giving the bread and the wine, recites the actual words of our Lord at the institution of the Sacrament. Which is significant, for the communicants thereby realize that the Sacrament is the Lord's, and that He is present to their faith and need. No word is spoken during the celebration. Everything, the simplicity and the silence alike, is intended to bring out the sacred, spiritual meaning of the Communion as the fellowship of the Lord with His people.

So the Church works in this Sacrament of Communion. But divine service is more than worship, and the fresh consecration and sense of brotherhood thus gained are to be worked out in the varied spheres of a Church's duty to the community and to the mission-field for which it is specially responsible. This implies a well-ordered fellowship, however, and to that we now turn.

CHAPTER IX

HOW A PRESBYTERIAN CHURCH WORKS

THE three executive courts of a Presbyterian Church are: (a) the Kirk-Session, or, as the French called it, the Consistory; (b) the Presbytery, or Classis or Colloquy; and (c) the Synods. Of the latter, the Provincial Synod is under the National Synod or General Assembly. There are minor variations and differences throughout the Churches. Thus in the Netherlands all the members of the Church in a city used to be considered as a single congregation, so that there was only one kirk-session or consistory for them all, i.e. it was not strictly a congregational court. Again, in France the Presbytery met only twice, ' or if possible four times ' a year, instead of monthly.

(a) The kirk-session consists of the minister and the elders; there must be at least two elders to form a session, over which only a minister can preside as moderator; for elders by themselves cannot constitute a meeting of session. Otherwise, all the members are equal, with the same right to discuss and to vote. The powers of the kirk-session are confined to the congregation which it represents; no kirk-session can interfere with another. Its main duties are the spiritual oversight of the congregation in question, to see that the

Word and the sacraments are duly administered, to supervise the admission of members, and to administer discipline. Through the kirk-session the congregation thus governs itself. The members are elected either by the session, who in certain cases nominate them, or by the congregation. They are usually ordained for life.[1] The large majority are, of course, laymen, but theological professors or ministers no longer in a charge who are members of the congregation may be also elected to a kirk-session, in which case, of course, they are not ordained. An elder cannot be a member of more than one kirk-session.

One important proviso is that if a kirk-session has any complaint against the minister of the congregation, it must bring this before the presbytery.

In the Westminster *Form of Church Government* it is enacted that

As there were in the Jewish Church elders of the people joined with the priests and Levites in the government of the Church, so Christ . . . hath furnished some in His Church, beside the ministers of the Word, with gifts for government, and with commission to execute the same, when called thereunto, who are to join with the minister in the government of the Church, which officers reformed Churches commonly call elders.

Whether these are meant in 1 Cor. xii. 28 (governments, helps), or in 1 Tim. v. 17, has been much debated by Presbyterian ecclesiastics. But no institution of the Presbyterian Churches has so admirably met the practical requirements of religious order and discipline.

[1] At first, in Scotland, they were annually elected. In the American Churches the rotary system is now popular, elders serving for three years.

The lay elders represent one of the important functions discharged by many under different names in the apostolic Church. They are commonly called ruling elders ('lay elders' is wrong), or, as Calvin termed them, *seniores plebis, gubermatores ex plebe delecti*, i.e. those who possess the gift of government. They represent the congregation in the kirk-session, and exercise government and discipline along with the minister there as well as in Synods and General Assemblies to which they may be sent as delegates.

Presbyterianism as it has evolved has confined the election of such elders to the Church itself. In the special conditions of the time, there was a tendency to allow the civil authorities, in a Christian State, to nominate in whole or part the board of elders who were to govern the Church. This was allowed under Lutheranism, although efforts were made here and there to secure the right of the Church to elect its own ruling elders. Even under Calvinism, for a time, concessions had to be made to the civil authorities. In Swiss Churches like those of Zurich and Geneva, the State as a municipally organized authority acted with the Church; indeed, the City Councils had some authority over the Synods, and this led to friction, as at Geneva, where Calvin had to uphold what he regarded as the spiritual independence of the Church against the restriction of elders to members of the City Councils. Nevertheless, the State here was not a persecuting opponent, as it was in France, where the consistories had a freer hand in developing their Presbyterian polity, and where the elders and deacons were chosen by the Church courts alone, the civil magistrates having neither part nor interest in the government of the Huguenot Church.

The French autonomy was reproduced in Scotland, and is now normative. Elders are elected or nominated by the local congregation, without outside interference ; they are then ordained by the minister and the kirk-session.

Presbyterianism does not require ' an atmosphere of comparative equality among the congregation, and an eldership chosen from the middle class '. With all respect to Mr. Trevelyan, one must deny this ; elders are chosen from all classes, from dukes to ditchers, in Scotland, and it is the glory of the Presbyterian polity everywhere, in its normal working, to draw upon the services of members in every rank and class. But it is true that there were elements in the Presbyterian scheme which proved ' uncongenial to the semi-feudal life of the English village. In the economic and social history of England the squire was still in the ascendant, the yeoman freeholder was about to decline, and the agricultural labourer could not, like the Scottish peasant, rise to the height of the argument of human equality, and attain through a democratic Church to self-reliance and self-respect '.[1] Even here ' democratic ' may be a misleading term, however. For Presbyterianism is not democratic, in the sense that the people dictate the belief and determine the polity of the Church ; it was and is ' democratic ' as it claims popular representation and self-government in opposition to episcopal prelacy and anything like an Erastian absolutism on the part of the State.

The fact that in the Presbyterian polity laymen have a recognized place in the courts of the Church and

[1] G. M. Trevelyan, *England under the Stuarts* (12th edition, 1925), p. 343.

administrative powers alike in doctrine and in discipline has led to a rich development of ability and devotion in the ranks of the eldership. The spirit of responsibility and of leadership is evoked in an unprecedented degree. It is on the efficiency of the elders that the Presbyterian Church in any community largely depends. The extent to which they take their duties seriously varies, as is only natural. But the opportunities and responsibilities of the office are calculated to draw out the best in a man, and it is remarkable how often, upon the whole, the eldership rises to its responsibilities. In every successful congregation, the living factors of fellowship and service include the loyalty of the office-bearers, who, by their character and standing, as well as by definite service in teaching the young or visiting their districts or carrying on religious and social work, give powerful support to the minister. They are associated with him in the administration of the Sacrament and in the varied responsibilities of the kirk-session. Often they are extremely busy men in trade and commerce and the learned professions. But their public spirit is freely put at the disposal of the Church, and in towns and country districts alike their contribution to its efficiency is one of its most valuable assets. Sometimes they are ahead of the ministers in initiative and enterprise; seldom are they far behind or long behind them.

(b) The presbytery is composed of all the ministers within the bounds, and of elders representing the various congregations. Commonly each congregation appoints yearly one representative elder, but in the United Free Church of Scotland a congregation with over four hundred and fifty communicants is permitted to send two. The presbytery elects one of its own ministers as moderator. Its functions are (*a*) judicial, in the sense that it deals with any appeals or petitions from kirk-sessions within its bounds, and supervises the proceedings of the lower courts. It also (*b*) supervises students for the ministry within its bounds, and ordains or admits ministers to vacant charges as well as theological professors to their chairs. As a court with representatives from every congregation within its bounds, the presbytery is able to supervise the whole work of the Church for which it is responsible, to aid weaker congregations, to initiate local enterprises of evangelism and service, and to prevent overlapping of agencies. It is the expression of co-operative loyalty and efficiency, and, where presbyteries are well organized, they are an invaluable aid to successful enterprise and a safeguard against anything like a selfish congregationalism.

A presbytery does consist of ministers and ruling elders, but the former are its standing members, whereas the ruling elders are simply delegates from the congregations who hold office for a given period. A presbytery may be validly constituted without any ruling elders being present, but no number of ruling elders could of themselves constitute a meeting of presbytery.

One habit has been discontinued. In the Book of Common Order it was enacted that ministers and elders should meet every Thursday, they they might ' diligently examine all such faults and suspicions as may be espied, not only amongst others, but chiefly among themselves '. Discipline, like charity, was to begin at home !

It was under the Commonwealth in seventeenth-century England that " classis " came to denote a presbytery, i.e. the group of ministers and elders in any given district.

K

This is the point of Milton's sneer in his irregular sonnet, where he complains of the " classic hierarchy " which the Presbyterians of the Westminster Assembly were endeavouring to force upon the English people. " Dare ye," he asks them indignantly,

> Dare ye to
> Ride as with a classic hierarchy ?

' Classic ! ' forsooth, he means, with a play on the term ' classical ' and on the sense of ' classis ' as a presbytery.

One important function is the supervision of theological students, throughout their course and at its close. When the theological training is over, for example, the student comes before the presbytery with his certificates and is set apart or licensed to preach the Gospel. He is then what is called a licentiate or ' probationer ', i.e. he is on probation, and has to commend his gifts to a vacant congregation. During the interval he may engage in any Church work, though he cannot dispense the sacraments ; often he learns experience by becoming assistant to some minister. Some of these probationers never receive a call. The classic book on this character is Dr. James Brown's *Life of a Scottish Probationer*, a charming piece of biography. Sir Walter Scott's sketch of Dominie Sampson, in *Guy Mannering*, was also based on fact, for in the older days, when the Church managed the education of the country, a probationer who failed to secure a call from any congregation might betake himself to a tutor's or schoolmaster's life. On the other hand, a licentiate may be elected to a professor's chair, without having held a ministerial charge. Professor Robertson Smith was thus elected by the Free Church.

This responsibility of the presbytery for theological

students is one of the few remaining channels connecting the British Churches with education. Count John of Nassau, in 1594, declared that sound education ' produces soldiers and patriots with a true knowledge of God and a Christian conscience ', adding, ' Churches and schools, good libraries, books and printing-presses are worth more than all the armies, arsenals, alliances, and treaties in the world.' Dr. A. W. Harrison, in citing this, comments : ' All the strength of Presbyterianism and much else in Dutch and Scottish history lie in these strong words.' [1] The belief in popular education was keen, from the start ; the Church in Geneva and the Netherlands and Scotland, especially, addressed itself to the betterment of schools, in order to train an intelligent people. With this went the insistence upon an educated ministry, which helps to explain the achievements in preaching. Nowadays the State has practically taken over the responsibility for popular education, though the Churches still have their interest in it, particularly in America, where the interest is active and enterprising to an extent unknown elsewhere. In all Churches, however, the training of the ministry remains intact. And a concern for this is laid upon the presbyteries in particular.

The Presbyterian Churches are still opposed to the admission of women to the presbyterate, but in some Churches, e.g. the Presbyterian Church of England and the Chinese Church, they are eligible for the eldership, or for the Deacons' Court, as in the United Free Church of Scotland and the (Southern) Presbyterian Church in the United States. The former Church, like the American, associates women with committees and

[1] *The Beginnings of Arminianism* (1926), p. 32.

boards appointed for special purposes. They are also carefully trained for service as Church Sisters in home mission work, as well as for educational and medical work in the foreign field. Women's Guilds and Girls' Guilds, as well as Young Men's Guilds, abound, and the organization of Women's Work in the Church of Scotland, largely owing to the initiative of Professor Charteris, has developed so richly that the ancient order of Deaconesses has been revived. The Deaconesses are specially trained and then set apart for their office. There are also Parish Sisters, appointed to organize work among women.

Here it is right to say a word about deacons. ' The whole policy of the Kirk consisteth in three things, in doctrine, discipline, and distribution.' So the *First Book of Discipline*, which recognized ministers, elders, and deacons as the statutory ministry of the Church. But it was not until the *Second Book of Discipline* (viii) that deacons were instituted as ' an order and perpetual ecclesiastical function in the Kirk of Christ ', and entrusted with the charge of the Church's finance, i.e. with the duty of distributing money for the care of the poor, with the supervision of collections and seat-rents and other funds for the upkeep of ministers and congregations, etc. But the ecclesiastical functions of deacons were never clear. At first they seem to have sat in the kirk-sessions, as was the practice of the French Church, and sometimes it was proposed that they should be allowed to vote in presbyteries. The office tended to wane, however, till it was occasionally revived in some of the seceding congregations during the eighteenth century. In the Free Church of Scotland after 1843 it was made a standing court of the Church, on the lines of the *Second Book of Discipline*, i.e. as a court whose members, as was the case at Geneva, could not become members of any higher court. In the Book of Common Order the office of deacons ' is to gather the alms diligently, and faithfully to distribute it, with the consent of the ministers and elders : also to provide for the sick and impotent persons, having ever a diligent care that the charity of godly men be not wasted upon loiterers and idle vagabonds '. This marks out the special responsibility and jurisdiction of the Deacons' Court, or, as it is in some Churches, the Board of Managers, who are often elected for a term of years. It is not necessary for a minister to preside over a meeting of the Deacons' Court. But when he is present, he presides. All elders are, in virtue of their office, members of the Court. And like the kirk-session, it is under the jurisdiction of the presbytery, to which its minutes have to be annually submitted. In the American Churches and in some others there is also a Board of Trustees for every congregation, who represent the Church as a corporation.

A Deacons' Court, therefore, has no share in the worship or discipline of the Church, but it is a spiritual court, inasmuch as the care of money and of the poor is for the Church a sphere of religious responsibility.

(c) Originally, i.e. in the *First Book of Discipline* (1560), the Synod was the Superintendent's Council, which corresponded to the Diocesan Synod of the bishop in the mediæval Church, but actually fulfilled almost the same functions as the Provincial Synod which had just been organized by the French Church, where the members chose their own moderator for their half-yearly meetings. The Synod, or Provincial Assembly, meets twice a year, partly to supervise the presbyteries, and partly to hear any appeals from them. It consists of the ministers within the bounds and of the representative elders in the various presbyteries, though in America any Synod is free to determine its own method of representation. A Synod elects its own moderator, and usually meets twice a year. The number of Synods naturally varies in proportion to the size and extent of the Church ; in each of the two great Scottish Churches there are sixteen, in the Presbyterian Church of the United States there are no fewer than forty. So far as authority goes, the Synod is inferior to the General Assembly ; it is the connecting-link between presbyteries and the Assembly, reviewing all the business of the former ; but an appeal can be taken from any decision of the Synod to the Assembly. At the same time it is competent for the Synod to call the attention of any presbytery to some matter of moment, and also to overture the Assembly on its own initiative.

In America, Canada, and England originally the Supreme Court was a Synod, not a General Assembly. Naturally, they vary in size ; but as a presbytery must have at least five congregations, so three presbyteries are the minimum for a Synod.

(d) The General Assembly is a representative court of the whole Church, annually elected. Different methods of election prevail, although their varieties have a fairly common aim. Thus, the presbyteries of the Presbyterian Church in the United States elect commissioners on the basis of one minister and one elder for every twenty-four ministers or any fraction over twelve in each presbytery. In the Church of Scotland, the Court is elected as follows : (a) ministers from presbyteries, one from every four (or part of four) in each presbytery ; (*b*) representative elders elected by the presbyteries, in the proportion of one to every six (or part of six) ministers ; and (*c*) representative elders from each of the four Universities and the sixty-nine royal burghs, with two from Edinburgh, the capital. In the United Free Church the number of elders is exactly the same as the number of ministers, and the number of such commissioners is about a third of the number of ministers on the presbyteries' roll.

The moderator is chosen by the Assembly itself ; he presides over its meetings, and constitutes the Assembly of the following year. During his year of office he also presides, as a rule, over the Commission of the Assembly, i.e. a special meeting later in the year which is appointed to deal with any particular items of business left over from the preceding Assembly.

Each Assembly is free to act for itself ; it is not bound by the decisions of previous Assemblies, unless these have become Acts of the Church, and, in order to prevent hasty legislation, it has been the custom in the Scottish Church, ever since 1697, to observe the Barrier Act, according to which no proposal of any General Assembly can become a law for the Church until it has been first sent down to all the presbyteries and received the consent of a majority. It was a doubtful decision on a case of this kind which precipitated the unhappy Secession of 1732 in the Church of Scotland.

The General Assembly reviews the whole work of the Church, on the basis of reports from every field of activity ; it also receives and discusses overtures sent up through presbyteries and Synods, and in particular it acts as a supreme court of appeal. Any complaints or petitions against decisions of presbyteries or Synods come before the General Assembly for final decision. It alone has the right to depose or to censure a minister, for example, as also to elect professors of theology, except when, as occasionally is the case in the Church of Scotland, such appointments in the University Divinity Faculties are otherwise made.

The General Assembly as the supreme council of the Church, has the power, upon occasion, and after the due forms of procedure have been observed, i.e. after consulting the Church through the lower courts, of declaring the catholic faith. It may restate its belief, or re-interpret its standards, to avoid misconception, and this is done in a corporate way, after full deliberation ; the Assembly in so acting claims to express the mind of the Church. From this it follows that the Assembly deals with any alleged heresies in its ministers or professors ; it has the supreme right and power of examining and pronouncing judgment upon any charges brought against them.

The services rendered by the General Assembly to the national life of Scotland have been already mentioned. As a debating court, it ranks high. But as a judicial body, it is sometimes less effective. So loyal a Presbyterian as Dr. Charles Hodge used to plead that such a large body could not act effectively as a court of appeal, and there have been notorious cases of wrong judgments, as when the Church of Scotland in 1831 deposed John McLeod Campbell for his book on *The Nature of the Atonement*—the one classic on this subject which Scotland has produced ; or when the Free Church suspended Professor Robertson Smith in 1881. But any popular assembly is liable to make such mistakes. On the whole, the percentage of hasty decisions is remarkably small. An Assembly commonly shows good judgment, and its records in the Presbyterian Church are for the most part very creditable.

The Presbyterian Church in the United States has found it needful to set up a very small General Council, since 1923, which resembles our Commission of Assembly, but which has powers of initiative and supervision ; the immense variety and range of the Church's activities require such a continuous body (of which the moderator is chairman), as well as four Boards of (i) National or Home Missions,[1] (ii) Foreign Missions, (iii) Christian Education, and (iv) Ministerial Relief and Sustentation. How necessary this organization is, may be guessed from the mere fact that while the population has increased twenty-one times since 1800, the membership of the Church has increased ninety times, throwing up problems of all kinds for a living Church which sets itself to keep abreast of the community's needs.

At the risk of underlining the obvious, I call attention to the fact that there is no court of the Church which is clerical. In the kirk-session the minister presides, but he is only one among the elders. In presbyteries, Synods, and General Assemblies, the numbers of clergymen and elders are practically the same. Hence there is no opportunity in a Presbyterian Church for clericalism in the English sense of the term. Even in the exercise of discipline or of solemn excommunication during former ages, it was not the minister who imposed his mind and will arbitrarily upon the people. The abuses

[1] This consists of thirty-six unpaid members, elected by the Assembly for three years ; twelve of them must be women.

of this exercise [1] may be singled out and ridiculed ; undoubtedly there was in Scotland as well as at Geneva an element of tyranny and of pettiness, an undue interference with personal liberties. But it is utterly unhistorical to describe this as clericalism or to compare it for a moment with the Spanish Inquisition ! Right or wrong, such exercises of Church power were actions of the Church through the minister. In the Scottish Book of Common Order, for example, it is expressly laid down that

if so be the congregation upon just cause agree to excommunicate, then it belongeth to the minister, according to their general determination, to pronounce the sentence, to the end that all things may be done orderly, and without confusion.

The point of this lies in the fact that the chief office of a minister has just been defined as standing ' in preaching the Word of God, and ministering the sacraments ; so that in consultations, judgments, elections, and other political affairs, his counsel, rather than authority, taketh place '.

These courts, we hold, express the conciliar rule of the Church effectively, fairly, and in a manner consonant with the principles of the apostolic Church. The humble Presbyterian, however, pays heed to the Scriptural proverb : ' Let another man praise thee, and not thine own mouth.' He recalls (to give but one testimony) what Jonathan Edwards wrote, on July 5,

[1] The cases of the Genevan and the Scottish Churches are generally used to exhibit the petty, intolerable methods of Church discipline ; the latter is drawn in a clever but one-sided fashion by Buckle in his *History of Civilization*, vol. iii. ch. 3, and by Dr. H. G. Graham in his *Social Life of Scotland during the Eighteenth Century*, chs. 8 and 9.

1750, to Dr. John Erskine of Edinburgh : 'As to the Presbyterian government, I have long been out of conceit with our unsettled, independent, confused way of Church government in this land ; and the Presbyterian way has ever appeared to me most agreeable to the Word of God and the reason and nature of things.

CHAPTER X

WORSHIP AND DEVOTIONAL LIFE

ALL these courts are constituted with prayer and devotional exercises. Which is no mere form. The spirit required for the working of the Church demands not simply business-like qualities, but the exercise of the virtues that belong to the Christian life, particularly good feeling, patience, and mutual consideration, as well as concern for the interests of the Church and the kingdom of God. But we now pass to a view of the worship and devotional life of the Churches, in its more distinctive features.

I

Worship, in the sense of the cultus, has been usually under the spell of the Calvinistic stress upon simplicity. The dominating aim has been to secure freedom and reverence, in accordance with the Word of God, and this has not been unsuccessful upon the whole. But simplicity has been too often identified with bareness. There has been a one-sided emphasis upon certain qualities of worship, and the recent developments of the Church have been in the direction of a larger recourse to relevant symbolism and to forms which might express devoutly and congenially the spirit of true worship.

Again I illustrate this from the history of the Scottish Churches, which is full of warning as well as of encouragement along this particular line. In the seventeenth century the Scottish Church gave up, out of deference to the English Independents, her ancestral liturgy or Book of Common Order. She took over from the Westminster Assembly a Directory for public worship.[1] It was intended to regularize worship in the Churches, providing ministers with suggestions for the conduct of public services, which should take the place of the Prayer Book. The latter, it was held, had fostered the growth of ' an idle and unedifying ministry, which contented itself with set prayers '. It was against such a position that Jeremy Taylor wrote his *Apology for Liturgy*, with its easy and damaging critique of the Directory. ' I can but with joy and eucharist ', he exclaimed, ' consider with what advantages and blessings the pious protestant is entertained, and blessed, and armed against all his needs, by the constant and religious usage of the Common Prayer Book.' But the Presbyterian leaders could not feel any such delight, and the result of their recoil was this manual. It perpetuates some of the weakest features in the earlier regulations for worship, within the reformed Scottish Church, e.g. the silencing of the people in prayer, and the small part assigned to praise or even to thanksgiving in the prayers. Indeed, the regulations of the *Directory for the Publick Worship of God* have long ceased to satisfy the fuller needs of devotional worship. But there are

[1] The story is told in Dr. Sprott and Dr. Leishman's edition of *The Book of Common Order and the Directory* (1868), and the best account of the Church of Scotland's practice lies in Dr. Sprott's *Worship and Offices of the Church of Scotland* (1882).

still some points which are none the worse for being pushed home to the conscience of our irreverent and casual generation. One is this :—

The publick worship being begun, the people are wholly to attend upon it, forbearing to read anything, except what the minister is then reading or citing ; and abstaining much more from all private whisperings, conferences, salutations, or doing reverence to any person present, or coming in ; as also from all gazing, sleeping, and other indecent behaviour, which may disturb the minister or people, or hinder themselves or others in the service of God.

Another counsel is : 'It is requisite that all the canonical books be read over in order.' The profit of a lectionary is thus recognized, but unluckily nothing was done to prevent the liberty of the minister in choosing lessons from Scripture from slipping into licence and reading at random.

One of the least unsatisfactory parts is that dealing with the Communion Service. The Directory gives a fine outline of the thoughts to be put before the congregation as they approach the Lord's Table. But this is really derived, and flattened in the course of transmission, from the Scottish Book of Common Order, known as Knox's Liturgy, which was used by the early Scottish Church. There the exhortation to be read by the minister before the Sacrament of Holy Communion contains these moving sentences :—

Albeit we feel in ourselves much frailty and wretchedness, in that we have not our faith so perfect and constant as we ought, being many times ready to distrust God's goodness through our corrupt nature ; and also that we are not so thoroughly given to serve God, neither have so fervent a zeal to set forth His glory, as our duty requireth, feeling still such rebellion in ourselves, that we have need daily to fight against the lusts of our flesh; yet nevertheless, seeing that our Lord hath dealt thus mercifully with us, that He hath printed His gospel in our hearts, so that we are preserved from falling into desperation and misbelief; and seeing also that He hath endued us with a will and desire to renounce and withstand our own affections, with a longing for His righteousness and the keeping of His commandments, we may now be right well assured that those defaults and manifold imperfections in us shall be no hindrance at all against us. . . . For the end of our coming thither is not to make protestation that we are upright or just in our lives; but contrariwise we come to seek our life and perfection in Jesus Christ. . . .

Let us consider, then, that this Sacrament is a singular medicine for all poor sick creatures, a comfortable help to weak souls, and that our Lord requireth no other worthiness on our part but that we unfeignedly acknowledge our naughtiness and imperfection.

The Lord's Supper, though intended to be a sacrament of fellowship, has proved a sad occasion of division among the Churches, and one instance of this occurred early in the history of the Scottish Church, when many objected to kneeling as they received the elements. This scruple had been felt strongly by John Knox, and it was specially cherished by those who resented the posture as one of the practices which King James VI enjoined, in order (as they feared) to conform the Scottish Church to the Anglican. But the real objection to kneeling as the communicants received the bread and the wine was that this had been associated with a superstitious adoration of the elements. Oddly enough, these conscientious objectors appear to have had Catholic tradition behind them, although they would have cared little or nothing for it even had they known it; the twentieth canon of the Council of Nicæa forbade kneeling and ordered standing at worship on Sundays. Dean Stanley, who points this out in his book on *Christian Institutions* (ch. iii), notes also that kneeling, which is our Western expression for reverence, does not correspond to the posture at the original Lord's Supper, which was reclining, and that sitting, ' the nearest approach in spirit, though not in form ', has disappeared from all Churches except two. ' The Presbyterian Churches receive the Communion sitting, by way of return to the old practice. The Pope for many centuries also received it sitting, probably by way of direct continuation from ancient times .'

It is an entire mistake to suppose that the Presbyterian Churches are committed to non-liturgical worship. From the first they had their native liturgies, on the Continent and in Scotland. But the same causes as had produced an antipathy to the use of any hymns in praise operated before long against any recourse to forms of prayer. The reaction against liturgies was partly due to an honourable but exaggerated devotion to freedom and spirit in worship, as though this was incompatible with the use of any forms of prayer, and partly to the fact that, as in the case of Scotland, the episcopal Church of Scotland sought to impose a new liturgy upon it, and thereby created a distaste for liturgies in general. It is a pity when minds work by reaction ; in Churches, as in individuals, it may sound strong, mainly because it goes readily into strong words, but it is a sign of weakness. Progress is not attained by recoiling as far as possible from what some other people hold, nor by discarding a practice incontinently either because it is being abused by contemporaries or because it has acquired some compromising associations. Unluckily, Presbyterians for a time parted with some precious elements of their heritage in worship, for reasons into which it is needless to enter here, and one of these was orderly, liturgical prayer, which like good music acquired odium from its connexion with episcopacy. It was for a long time believed that spontaneous, unpremeditated prayer was more inspired than any carefully drawn up collect. Even the use of the Lord's Prayer has been tabooed!

These sad days are over. In America so stout a Presbyterian churchman as Dr. Charles Hodge advised ' the optional use of a liturgy, or form of public service, having the sanction of the Church.'[1] This was in 1855, and it has been acted upon. Already, in the French Church, the brilliant ministry of M. Bersier in Paris had produced a similar reform in the direction of devotional order. In Scotland the pioneer was Dr. Robert Lee, minister of Old Grey Friars Church in Edinburgh, who encountered vehement opposition. A reconciling word was spoken in last century by the Duke of Argyll : ' That liturgical prayer should be used exclusively in religious worship, seems to me as unfortunate as that it should not be used at all.'[2] Like a number of reconciling words, this has not carried very far. But it is becoming more and more recognized that we are as free to use forms and prayer as to do without them in our worship. As a result of this slow and difficult revival, there is now, at any rate in Scotland, a welcome variety and wealth of worship, from the simple, most impressive service of a small congregation to the more

[1] *The Church and its Polity*, p. 161.
[2] *Presbytery Examined* (second edition), p. 290.

L

elaborate worship in our cathedrals, abbeys, and larger churches.

In France the Presbyterian movement was carried forward by waves of song. Church music came to the lips of the Huguenots, who, like their fellows in Germany and Britain, felt the new joy of being able to sing as well as to pray in their own vernacular. It was Clement Marot the French poet and courtier, who first translated some of the psalms into French, so effectively that they were sung to popular airs at the French Court. A complete edition of the Psalms ' *mis en rime Françoise* ' was published by Beza and himself for the worship at Geneva. Louis Bourgeois was the chief musician of the movement. For sixteen years he lent powerful aid to Calvin in Geneva. Indeed, it has been actually claimed that ' historians who wish to give a true philosophical account of Calvin's influence at Geneva ought probably to refer a great part of it to the enthusiasm attendant on the pleasure of singing Bourgeois's melodies '.[1] But Calvin's ideas of Church music were too narrow for his precentor in the end. Besides, the singing was unluckily narrowed to the Psalms of David.

The Scots had at first a chance of possessing a richer praise than their Continental fellows. Like the others, they delighted in singing to God in the vernacular, and at the dawn of the Reformation a number of ballads and hymns began to circulate, which were afterwards collected under the title of *The Good and Godly Ballads*. The man who edited them and wrote some of them was Robert Wedderburn, a Dundee citizen and priest, who joined the Reformers. This collection includes translations from the German, versions of psalms, and

[1] Dr. Robert Bridges, in *The Yattendon Hymnal*, p. 9.

adaptations of popular ballads, as was not uncommon.
There was no idea yet of confining the godly to the
Psalms of David. A rude, frank note sounds in some
of them. But what is most characteristic is a twofold
thrill. First, these Scots sang like men who had been
delivered. In the delight of the open air and the sun-
light into which they felt that they had escaped, they
adapted hunting songs and popular ballads to express
the joy that spread from shire to shire throughout the
land. Thus one gleeful song opened :—

> The Pope, that pagan full of pride,
>   He has us blinded long ;
> For where the blind the blind do guide,
>   No wonder they go wrong ;
> Like prince and king he led the ring
>   Of all iniquity :
>   Hey trix, tryme go trix,
>   Under the greenwood tree !

' The hunt is up ', sang others ; the cruel fox is being
hunted down this bright morning.

> The hunter is Christ, that hunts in haste,
>   The hounds are Peter and Paul,
> The Pope is the fox, Rome is the rocks,
>   That rubs us on the gall.

The other note is devotion to Christ as a personal Redeemer, which thrills through stanzas like
these :—

> Who has my heart but heaven's King ?
> Who causes me for joy to sing ?
> Whom that I love above all thing ?
>   Christ has my heart alway.

For us that blessed Bairn was born,
For us He was both rent and torn,
For us He crowned was with thorn :
  Christ has my heart alway.

For us He shed His precious blood,
For us He nailed was on the Rood,
For us He in many a battle stood :
  Christ has my heart alway.

Next Him, to love His mother fair,
With stedfast heart for evermair ;
She bore the birth, freed us from care :
  Christ has my heart alway.

Or in these :—

Down by yon river I ran,
  Down by yon river I ran,
Thinking on Christ so free,
Who brought me to liberty,
  And all for the love of man.

Who should be my love but He,
That alone has saved me,
  And by His death me won ;
On the cross so cruelly,
He shed His blood abundantly,
  And all for the love of man.

I cry and I call to Thee,
  Leave me not, leave me not ;
I cry and I call to Thee,
  Leave me not alone ;
All they that laden be,
Thou bidst them come to Thee ;
Then shall they saved be,
  Through Thy mercy alone.

> For love of One I make my moan
> > Right secretly,
> To Christ Jesu, that Lord most true,
> > For His mercy.
> O Lord who wrought all things of nought,
> > Grant me Thy mercy . . .
> Thy humble word, with one accord,
> > Let be restored
> To sinners all, when they do call
> > For Thy mercy.

This verse is from a hymn called ' A gentle admonition of Christ ' :—

> All people, learn of Me
> Gentleness and piety :
> Remember My suffering body,
> So wounded and bloody :
> Kill no man unkindly
> > With slander nor with pain :
> Amend your faults daily,
> > And from vice refrain.

The Good and Godly Ballads, for all their defects, are charged with natural joy and hope.

> We should love God and merry be,
> And drive away despair.

This was a practical fulfilment of the New Testament counsel, ' Is any merry ? let him sing psalms.' But ere long the narrower view of the Word of God being the standard of what was to be sung in the Scottish Churches fell upon the country, and the early lilt of heartfelt piety was silenced. It took the Scottish Churches much longer time than the American to have their full rights to the range of sacred song recognized. For long, for too long, the praise became confined to the singing of metrical versions of the Psalms of David. It was supposed, though this is now known to be a mistake, that the primitive Christians sang nothing but these psalms, and since it was the rule that worship should be according to the Word of God, all hymns were ejected eventually from the service of praise. Even the Scripture Paraphrases, which came to be attached to the Scottish Psalter, were finally regarded by some as human inventions and excluded from use. They are still ignored by some congregations in the Scottish Highlands. It was not until the end of the eighteenth century that the Churches began to take a larger view of praise, at least in Scotland. The credit belongs to the Relief Church. The Seceders, indeed, committed themselves to the notion that ' to introduce hymns of human composition, or even paraphrases, in which undue liberties are taken with the original text, tends to endanger the purity both of the worship and doctrine of the Church '. But in 1794 the Relief Church ventured to publish a small hymn-book. This lead was eventually followed by the more conservative Churches in the country. The revised edition of *The Church Hymnary*, which is issued this year, represents real progress both in music and in words. It has been prepared by representatives of the Churches of Scotland, England, Wales, and Ireland, and is also authorized for use in the Churches of Australia, New Zealand, and South Africa, the American and the Canadian Churches having already books of their own. The Hymnary thus is an international manual. It is thoroughly catholic in its range and taste, including hymns ancient and modern, with the Canticles, the Apostles' and the Nicene Creeds, etc. With the publication of this book the Presbyterian Churches of to-day have taken their place in the forefront of hymnology, after the long delay and hesitation of the past two centuries.

Our most famous hymn-writer is Dr. Horatius Bonar of the Free Church of Scotland, in last century; his hymns have gone round the world, and a number of them are a lasting possession of Christian worship. Other hymnists—to pick out only one or two of them—are Mrs. Prentniss, the American authoress of ' More love to Thee, O Christ '; Dr. Duffield, also an American, who wrote ' Stand up, stand up for Jesus '; Dr. Philip Schaff of New York, notable as a translator of Latin hymns ; Dr. George Matheson, famous for his hymn ' O Love that wilt not let me go'; and Welshmen like Morgan Rhys, David and Thomas Charles, and David Morris. The list might be increased easily, but I exclude living writers. The Presbyterian contribution to the hymns of the world is not inconsiderable by any means, but it is not nearly as rich as the Anglican or even as the Independent or the Methodist contribution. And still in some of the smaller, more conservative Churches, Scottish and American, the psalms are the sole means of praise.

II

In devotional literature the Presbyterian Churches have not made any striking contribution. The life of the Church has been nourished through the ages upon more books than the Bible. But the adherence of the

Presbyterians to the Word of God, while it has had its advantages, has not been without its drawbacks, as we have already had occasion to notice in the sphere of worship. We have produced no books like the *De Imitatione Christi*, or *The Pilgrim's Progress*, or *The Christian Year*. Whatever be the reason, our literary output has not yielded any book which has taken its place in the devotional literature of the wide world, that is to say, if we except some hymns.

It is otherwise with theology. I wish I could have included the chapter I had planned upon the contribution of the Presbyterian Churches to theology, especially to dogmatic theology and apologetic and the philosophy of religion as well as to Biblical criticism. This has been exceptionally rich, so rich indeed that it would require far more space to treat it adequately than is available here. Reluctantly I must leave this aspect out of the picture. Still, even within the province of devotional literature our record is not quite barren. I shall mention two significant items. First, the Heidelberg Catechism, a remarkable sixteenth-century production,[1] composed by two young scholars whom the Elector Frederick had gathered round him at Heidelberg, to further the Calvinistic movement in the University and in the town, during the years 1561–1576. It was soon translated into Latin, Dutch, French, and English, and has since then passed into many other tongues. No catechism has such lyrical beauty and insight in dealing with the Christian experience ; as a devotional expression of Calvinism at its best, this little work deserves to be circulated and

---

[1] It is still the principal creed of the Reformed Church in the United States, founded in 1726 by Swiss and German immigrants.

read still. There are many editions in this country
and in America, one of the most convenient being that
issued by Dr. Alexander Smellie in the ' Books of the
Heart ' series (Andrew Melrose, London, 1890).

It begins :—

What is thy only comfort in life and death ? That I,
with body and soul, both in life and in death, am not
my own but belong to my faithful Saviour Jesus Christ,
who with His precious blood has fully satisfied for all my
sins, and redeemed me from all the power of the devil,
and so preserves me that, without the will of my Father
in heaven, not one hair can fall from my head, yea, that
all things must work together for my salvation. Where-
fore, by His Holy Spirit, He also assures me of eternal
life, and makes me willing and ready from my heart
henceforth to live unto Him.

The articles of the Apostles' Creed are included in the
summary of doctrine. Thus Question 55 is, ' What dost
thou understand by the *communion of saints* ? ' The
answer is : ' First, that believers, all and each, as
members of Christ, have part in Him and in all His
treasures and gifts ; secondly, that each one must feel
himself bound to use his gifts, readily and cheerfully,
for the advantage and welfare of other members .'
The ten commandments are also included and explained.
Thus, in reply to the question what doth God require
in the eighth commandment, it is said : ' That I further
my neighbour's good, where I can and may, deal with
him as I would have others deal with me, and labour
faithfully, that I may be able to help the poor in their
need.'

This particular interpretation of the eighth commandment, by the way, entered into the social side of the
Scottish Church at a later period. The honourable

connexion of humanitarian reform and evangelical religion was illustrated after 1843, when the Free Church addressed itself to the social problem. Theologically that Church was traditional as yet. No breath of liberalism stirred it. But in the midst of its own financial responsibilities, raising money to build churches and manses and schools, it did not forget the needs of the country; the impulse of Dr. Chalmers [1] was felt strongly in this sphere of activity. For some years there was a special committee of the Church entrusted with the care of housing schemes for the working classes. Money was collected and legislation was promoted, in the interests of better housing for the poor of Scotland. Dr. Begg was the leader of this movement, and when he was met, as such leaders have been often met, by the criticism that this was not spiritual work, he quoted the teaching of the Shorter Catechism. Did not the eighth commandment require 'the lawful procuring and furthering the wealth and outward estate of ourselves and others'? He properly declined to confine the spiritual functions of the Church to preaching and worship; they must run out into all practical concerns that attacked the problems of immorality and disease, especially in the large towns and cities of the land. So the work went happily forward. Professor Blaikie of the New College in Edinburgh, for example, was the author of a book on *Better Days for Working People* (1863), and Dr. Thomas Guthrie's noble work for education and for ragged schools in

[1] Chalmers's two papers on Poor Relief have been reprinted by modern economists in *Dr. Chalmers and the Poor Law* (Edinburgh, 1911), and Mr. N. Masterman gives extracts from his social studies in *Chalmers on Charity* (London, 1900), so fruitful were this Church leader's views on economics.

Edinburgh was one signal example of this social application of the Gospel.

However, to return to the Heidelberg Catechism. It closes with a section on Prayer, beginning with the question, 'Why is prayer needful for Christians?', the answer being 'Because it is the chief part of the thankfulness which God requireth of us, etc.' Then follows the Lord's Prayer, the final question being, 'What is the meaning of the word *Amen*?' '*Amen* means: So shall it truly and surely be. For my prayer is much more certainly heard of God than I feel in my heart that I desire these things of Him.'

Another treatise, the *Letters* of Samuel Rutherford, has won a wider vogue. Rutherford was Professor of Divinity in St. Andrews University about the middle of the seventeenth century. He had written in 1642 a *Peaceable and Temperate Plea for Paul's Presbyterie in Scotland*, which is, it must be confessed, more alliterative in its title than convincing in its arguments. He was the author of *Lex Rex*, which is pronounced by Dr. Taylor Innes to be one of the few important books upon constitutional law which Scotland has produced. But he also wrote letters to his friends, which have been collected and often edited for modern use. They are the nearest parallel in our literature to St. Bernard's *Sermones in Cantica Canticorum*. Here we have a scholar and churchman pouring out his soul in rhapsodical descriptions of Christ and the Christian life. There is an authentic fragrance in them, though it is too hot for our modern taste occasionally. No book of our Churches exhibits so strikingly as these *Letters* that inward and mystical devotion to Christ, which is the property of no one Church. And this rose sprang from the thorns of the seventeenth century, with its bitter clash between the Presbyterian Churches and the State, indeed between the Presbyterian Churches and all the others.

Dr. Andrew Murray, of the Dutch Reformed Church in last century, won international gratitude for his evangelical works ; he was a saintly character, and there was, there still is, a vogue for his devotional treatises.

III

A Church, however, may be better or worse than it seems on paper. It is best judged by its inner life and actual practice ; these yield a fairer sketch of its Christian temper than any manuals of devotion or formulation of ideals or programme of polity. So far as the Scottish Churches are concerned, it is possible to obtain some glimpses of this practical devotion through literature, and to watch the habits and tempers of the ministers and people living under the Presbyterian rule of life. I put down these scattered notes, by way of illustration. They are quite incomplete, of course, but they may be suggestive.

The sterling seventeenth-century piety of the Seceding Churches appears in Sir J. M. Barrie's Scottish idylls ; their subsequent religious life may be felt in Carlyle's description of his father (in the first volume of his *Reminiscences*), and further accounts, written from a sympathetic standpoint, are to be found in Dr. Woodside's *Soul of a Scottish Church* and in Dr. J. H. Leckie's recent *Secession Memories*, though Dr. John Brown's essays in *Horæ Subsecivæ* and Dr. A. R. Macewen's biography of Principal John Cairns are not to be for-

gotten, any more than the biography of John Brown of
Haddington. On the other side, the finer type of
Moderate minister makes his appearance in Ian Mac-
laren's Scottish idylls, for although Dr. John Watson
was born and bred within the Free Church, he never
concealed his admiration for parish ministers like Dr.
Barty of Bendochy. Dr. Carlyle of Inveresk's *Autobiography*, again, gives excellent hints about the state
of things round and within Edinburgh towards the close
of the eighteenth century; but it can hardly be called
an inspiring book, so far as the interests of personal
religion are concerned. The fibre of the Church's better
ministers, during the eighteenth century, with their
gracious Calvinism and readiness to be reasonable and
charitable, has never been better drawn than in the
picture of Dr. John Erskine, Dr. Robertson's colleague
in Greyfriars Church, Edinburgh, as sketched by Scott
in the thirty-seventh chapter of *Guy Mannering*. *The
Heart of Midlothian* and *Rob Roy*, with *Old Mortality*,
touch both the Covenanting and the opposite sides of
Church piety, and the parish ministers in *The Antiquary*
and in *St. Ronan's Well* answer to their fellows in
Galt's Ayrshire novels. The pastoral skill of Hender-
land, an eighteenth-century Highland catechist, is drawn
aptly by Stevenson in the sixteenth chapter of *Kid-
napped*. Stevenson's poems, *A Lowden Sabbath Morn*,
Embro Hie Kirk, and *The Scotsman's Return from
Abroad*, hit off in the main the Seceding type of
religion, whereas Burns touched the abuses of the
Church as he saw it in Ayrshire, in poems like
The Holy Fair, *The Ordination*, and *Holy Willie's
Prayer*, the last-named being 'the thirteenth chapter
of First Corinthians and the fifth chapter of St.

Matthew put into Scottish sarcasm '. [1]   But his
' priest-skelping turns ' in verse are balanced by the
picture of peasant family worship in *The Cottar's
Saturday Night*. The northern part of the country is
visible through Dr. Norman Macleod's *Reminiscences of
a Highland Parish*, and, from a different angle, in
Hugh Miller's fascinating autobiography, *My Schools and
Schoolmasters*, which contains many sidelights upon
religious life during the first half of last century. The
reaction against the rigid, morose Calvinism of Aber-
deenshire during the middle of last century is depicted
in the Scottish tales of George MacDonald. Dr. Alexander's *Johnnie Gibb of Gushetneuk*, published in 1871,
shows a less disturbed Church life in that district. His
Notes and Sketches (1877) bring out rural religious life
faithfully and pleasantly. Later in the century the
same reaction against traditional Calvinism is reflected
in the poems of Dr. Walter C. Smith, which mark the
rise of religious culture over the sectarian preoccupations
of the age.

It is by consulting such books that one often comes
upon a truer estimate of the devotional methods and
tempers of the people than in any other quarter. Reti-
cence has characterized our land as a rule in religion.
For example, during the last half of the nineteenth
century, when history books would suggest that the
country was absorbed in ecclesiastical controversy,
every man's hand against his neighbour, there must
have been hundreds of quiet, God-fearing people like
the ' old Scotch Gardener ', of whom R. L. Stevenson
writes in his *Memories and Portraits*. ' One thing was

[1] Dr. L. Maclean Watt, in *Scottish Life and Poetry*, pp. 400,
401.

noticeable about Robert's religion : it was neither dogmatic nor sectarian. He never expatiated (at least, in my hearing) on the doctrines of his creed, and he never condemned anybody else. I have no doubt that he held all Roman Catholics, Atheists, and Mahometans as considerably out of it ; I don't believe he had any sympathy for Prelacy ; and the natural feelings of man must have made him a little sore about Free Churchism ; but at least he never talked about these views, never grew controversially noisy, and never openly aspersed the belief or practice of anybody.' Nor did he talk in the open about personal religion.

Of all Churches this was true, in different ways. There was no homogeneous type of religious feeling and conduct, but the Presbyterian worship and traditions did produce what may be considered a fairly distinctive type, under the variations of Celtic and Lowland culture. Not all the devout were taken up with the affairs of the Kirk and the State, like the Laird o' Cockpen. And even those who were, had often a deep current of quiet devotion and loyalty, which rarely emerged to advertise itself in public. ' Godliness ' rather than what is termed ' saintliness ' suits it best.

CHAPTER XI

TO-DAY AND TO-MORROW

' IF it was hard to believe in a moving earth ', said Tyrrell, ' it is harder to believe in a moving Church.' But it is by the hard things that one lives, not by the easy things that require a mere acquiescence. And the hard things become easier as they are faced. The Church lives and moves, moves because it lives and as it lives ; however disturbing and unwelcome this may be, there is no profit in ignoring it, much less in declining to realize what it involves in thought and practical service. I wish now to suggest how the Presbyterian Churches appear at present in the light of this generalization.

Movement does not necessarily mean change. It may simply denote activity. But activity involves mental effort, and this, in a moving order of providence, may demand re-interpretation of belief and openness to fresh ideals of service, in order to render the witness of the Church adequate. The Presbyterian Churches have moved, as we have already seen, sometimes almost against their will. They are moving and are bound to move further in some directions, if they are to be true to their traditions and their opportunities in the present, just as they continue to be moved by the Spirit of God to whom they owe their loyalty and life.

' L'histoire est un vaste cimetière ', said a French statesman the other day in the Chamber of Deputies ; ' s'il est bon d'y aller, il ne faut pas s'y attacher.' But, M. Briand, suppose history is something else ? Suppose it is not a cemetery but a church, where you may find memorials of the dead past, and yet where the living are baptized and married and inspired for to-day and to-morrow? This is the conception of history which has underlain the preceding pages. In terms of it I proceed to inquire how the rising generation of Presbyterians are likely to carry on the family tradition, even although their speech and dress and dwellings are not invariably those of their great ancestors.

I

The high Church claims of spiritual independence once made by Presbyterians, and notably by Scottish Presbyterians during the course of their struggles, have been sometimes dubbed Presbyterian Hildebrandism. Historically, they were put now and then in forms which were untenable. In the conflict with Stuart absolutism, the assertion of the Church's freedom seemed to endanger the Constitution, as it set up an uncontrolled State within the State. Through such passions and prejudices the Church has been forced into a saner expression of its jurisdiction. ' The essence of Hildebrandism ', as Principal Rainy put it once, ' is to assert that the Church's decision ought to bind the State's conscience, and so decide the State's action.'[1] Whereas Presbyterian churchmen would hold that, while the State is not to assume any Erastian relation to the

[1] In his *Three Lectures on the Church of Scotland*, pp. 96–99.

M

Church, dictating its worship or creed or polity, yet it is not bound to accept any ' authoritative decision from the Church. . . . The State is to take notice that a society has been set up, by no human authority, in which exist duties, privileges, relations, based solely on the common recognition, in conscience of a common Lord. What is done in this society takes effect, not by force, but simply by the power that conviction and conscience happen to have in the minds of those concerned. . . . The State should give full and equitable effect to the principle that such a society has the right to exist, and to do its own work according to its conscience. If the State will not give effect to this reasonable principle, the society will still do its own work, not minding the State, carrying its decisions in the strength of its own spiritual resources. . . . But the State is acknowledged to retain all its rights and powers, whether it is Christian or not. Surely this is something different from Hildebrandism.' It is. Our Churches have moved forward to this position. But one must frankly admit that such was not the full claim which the Presbyterian Churches made or were supposed to be making in the heyday of their struggles, for example, with Stuart absolutism, when the divine right of kings, which in essence aimed at the divine rights of civil government and independence of the papacy, clashed with the divine right of Presbytery, to the confusion of both. Fortunately the historical exigencies that led to such a document as *The Solemn League and Covenant* have long since passed away. That issue is extinct. It would be absurd to say that the modern State in any country could not take up a position which might oblige the Presbyterian Church once more to raise the

old cry about the Crown Rights of the Lord Jesus
Christ within His Church being endangered. It was
indeed the sense that an intolerant democracy in
Switzerland did encroach upon the liberties of the Church
that led Vinet and his friends in 1847 to found ' L'Eglise
Libre du Canton de Vaud '. It is conceivable that
democratic autocracy or bureaucracy might reopen
the controversy once more. Still, on the whole, in
these days of religious toleration, the freedom of the
Church, as vindicated reasonably by Presbyterian
churchmen, appears to be as secure as anything is
secure in the present order, European or non-European.
' We hold ', Principal Hill declared,[1] ' that no particular
form of Church government is so precisely marked
down in Scripture, as to render any other unlawful.
There are general rules to which all that bear office in
the Church of Christ are required to conform, whatever
be their name or their distinctions of rank. But these
rules admit of that variety in the forms of Church
government, by which the religion of Jesus is qualified
to receive the countenance and protection of all the
possible forms which civil government can assume.'
Theoretically that may be accurate, although the
Principal's closing words would sound optimistic to our
Presbyterian churchmen to-day in lands like Chosen or
Lithuania or Transylvania or Russia, where civil government can be uncivil enough.

The interest of this aspect is mainly historical for
us. At the same time, misguided and fanatical as were
the forms into which the Presbyterian Churches sometimes put their claims of independence, the sharp intolerance and the constitutional perils of it ought not

[1] *Lectures in Divinity*, ii. 548.

to obscure the fact that these churchmen were right in maintaining that the State was not possessed of a jurisdiction which could make light of the individual conscience or of the Church as a religious community with rights and powers which no civil authority could either grant or deny. So long as toleration was impracticable, it was a service to truth and freedom for the Church to assert its supremacy in matters of faith, and even to counsel the State on such matters ; otherwise, the State would have relapsed into the older and fatal position of claiming to proclaim as well as to enforce what it considered to be true religion. Better, at any rate, that it should be told to take its orders in such a sphere from the Church. This was not the best position, but it was on the way to the best. Dr. J. N. Figgis, who recognizes this, admits [1] that ' the claims of Pope or Presbyter to control the secular power in the interests of the spiritual enshrined in the only form possible to those times, the principle of *the rights of conscience* '. He does not realize the difference between the claims of Pope and Presbyter ; apparently he thinks, like some to whom I have already referred, that Presbyterianism is one form of clericalism. But he does see the element of justice in the claim, although he drops, not undeservedly, hard words upon the latter. The point is that this contention, with the just claim of spiritual freedom at the heart of it, was carried forward and worked out principally by Presbyterian churchmen ; the brunt of the struggle fell upon them, largely because they were a Church, and as such felt

[1] *The Divine Right of Kings*, pp. 213, 214. Were I a bishop, I would not allow any clergyman in my diocese to utter a word upon Church and State until he had mastered this treatise

their duties over against the State whose claims had to be delimited. Other Christian bodies argued the question, but in the course of providence it fell to the Churches of Geneva, Holland, and Scotland to show how the vital claims of the Church as a national organization had to be taken into account and treated with due respect. Out of it all has come the idea and vision, at least, not of a sect, but of a Church truly free within its own province, yet co-operating with the State for the highest welfare of the country.

II

It is this consciousness of being a Church which explains what seems rather disconcerting at the present day, the not infrequent reluctance of Presbyterians to merge themselves with their fellow-Christians in some new and larger body for the ends of the kingdom of God. Here and there, even in the foreign mission-field, it has been the Presbyterians who have proved the obstacle to a federation of the local Churches. The opposition may not always spring entirely from the highest of motives. But in most cases, where it is sincere, it will be found to have an ecclesiastical root. I do not use the term ' ecclesiastical ' in any disparaging or depreciatory sense ; at its highest, it means a belief in the Church and the ministry as vital to the being as well as to the well being of Christianity. Such a belief is bound to determine the policy of the Church. Thus (a) the fundamental article of the parity of presbyters prevents reunion with episcopal Churches, if episcopacy be interpreted as prelacy, which infringes the apostolic function of the Christian ministry as

Presbyterians have learned to recognize these. On the other hand (*b*), our belief in the ministry implies a divine commission, with ordination by ministers of the Church, and this in turn may prove a difficulty when a Presbyterian Church is invited to unite with Christians who conscientiously hold lower views of the ministry. In neither case need the obstacle be insuperable. But they are real, as anyone will understand who has followed the negotiations, for example, with regard to the recent Lambeth Conference in England—one of the most broad-minded pronouncements of our generation, or the ecclesiastical sequel to the formation of the great United Church of Canada in 1925. This is no place to enter into such debates and differences. I merely mention them in order to bring out the truth that we Presbyterian churchmen had better not blur our principles, even while we desire and plan to do as much as in us lies to heal the wounds of our divided Christendom.

Thus we would yield to none in our recognition of the historical services rendered to the Church by the diocesan episcopate. We admire without hesitation or reserve the character of many individual prelates, down to the present day. But when we are asked to believe that this episcopate acquired or inherited the right to monopolize authority over the Church, apart from presbyters, to ordain presbyters in virtue of some special apostolic commission, as though presbyters could not fulfil their ministerial functions except in virtue of a gift transmitted by the episcopate, and to confirm catechumens, our firm reply would be that, while we reverence use and wont, '*Nolumus leges ecclesiæ apostolicæ mutari*'. On this issue we stand to-day where our forefathers stood yesterday. As far back as

the seventeenth century François de Gaultier of Mont-
pellier, moderator of the last Synod of Bas-Languedoc
in 1681, who published a *Histoire apologétique ou Defense
des libertés des Églises réformées de France* (1688), submitted to King James II a project for reunion between
Anglicans and Presbyterians.   He was one of the many
French Huguenots who had no objection to episcopacy
as an office of discipline and order.[1]   But he frankly
laid down this proviso : ' On ne dira plus que l'épiscopat
soit de droit devin, on n'obligera plus les pasteurs à la
réordination.'   And it was on this rock that in England
the contemporary attempts to unite Episcopalians and
Presbyterians were wrecked.   The former clung to the
novelty of episcopacy as divinely constituted and as
the one valid source of authority, the guarantee of a
valid ministry.   The Presbyterians were not unwilling
to meet them on the original ground of English episcopacy, but they could not allow that the apostolic
functions of the ministry were not fully entrusted to
presbyters as such.   Nor are we.   ' *L'Église réformée
est toujours réformable*', as M. Pannier puts it, provided
that its fundamental principles are conserved.   It is
fundamental to the Presbyterian Church that presbyters
are fully qualified by their apostolic commission to
ordain, to administer the sacraments, to ' take heed to
themselves and to all the flock, in which the Holy Spirit
has made them bishops ', and, in conjunction with
ruling elders, as representing the Church, to supervise
and serve the Christian fellowship.   This is the salient

[1] An interesting collection of testimonies and opinions from
French Huguenots, more or less representative, is printed by
M. Jean Pannier in the *Revue d'Histoire et de Philosophie
Religieuses* (1926), pp. 434–470.

point for Presbyterians ; they do not cling to the parity of presbyters merely because they are a set of religious levellers, obsessed by a doctrinaire action of equality.

If it be impossible, however, in the present circumstances, to reach and recover a representative, constitutional episcopate which will do full justice to the apostolic functions of presbyters, it is not impossible for Presbyterians to secure some equivalent for the services of order and discipline which a diocesan bishop, discharging his pastoral and fatherly office aright, confers upon his brethren. Every active and progressive community, social or religious, involves a certain pre-eminence for some of its members, no matter how democratic the organization may be. It is, indeed, pre-eminence in and for service. Only where it is abused for the sake of ambition or greed, is it ever resented by sensible and devoted men. The apostolic Church itself had its Diotrephes, ' who loveth to have the pre-eminence '. He had to be dealt with by John the presbyter. Whether he was a presbyter or not, we cannot tell ; but his sons have abounded in the Presbyterian Churches as in all others. On the other hand, a Christian pre-eminence accrues to certain men naturally. The Presbyterian system not only permits but requires presbyters who become, in one department or another, responsible to the Church for maintaining order, managing business, and giving a lead. Men like Bucer at Strassburg during the sixteenth century were the prototypes of many in the later Presbyterian Churches, who were bishops in all but the official name. The parity of ministers is not equivalent to a mechanical equality. By force of character and natural ability, some are born to be leaders, and in any Presbyterian Church there are more

or less unofficial positions for such men, to whom their
fellows are proud to defer and to look up. Furthermore,
there are secretaries and officials set apart for administrative purposes in every department. The ancient
rank of superintendent, for example, was revived, to
all intents and purposes, when Dr. James Robertson of
Winnipeg assumed his splendid position as director of
the North-West Home Mission propaganda in the
Canadian Church from 1881 to 1902. A man like this
is *primus inter pares*, and the *pares* are the better for
his Christian primacy.

All this belongs, however, to the internal working of
our system. As for the larger question, all that needs
to be said is that in discussions upon Church reunion
in any country, and in the practical rearrangements
that may follow these, the Presbyterian Churches have
and will continue to have a difficult duty. They hold
a definite view of the Church and the ministry, as I
have tried to indicate. This forms no obstacle to close,
active co-operation with other Churches or Christian
associations for common ends of religious or social
welfare. But when it comes to forming an organic
union, questions may be raised to which the Presbyterian
Churches, if they are to be faithful to the convictions
and principles of their catholic heritage, must not
shrink from giving definite answers, and from seeking
to secure, in no sectarian spirit, that the essence of such
principles be somehow conserved.

III

Are the Presbyterian Churches moving towards
Creed Revision ? It is specially a living question for

them, as their traditional standard is the Westminster Confession of Faith, which has been already re-interpreted in almost all Churches on the issue of toleration, the common attitude being to disclaim all persecuting and intolerant principles. Thus, in Scotland, in order to remove ' difficulties and scruples felt by some ' as to the ' teaching or supposed teaching ' of the Westminster Confession, the United Presbyterian Church in 1879 and the Free Church in 1892 passed Declaratory Acts, repudiating all persecuting principles, and setting in the forefront ' the love of God to all mankind ', denying that ' any who die in infancy are lost, or that God may not extend His grace to any who are without the pale of ordinary means, as it may seem good in His sight ', and modifying the doctrine of total depravity. The Free Church declared that she did not consider ' her office-bearers, in subscribing the Confession, committed to any principles inconsistent with liberty of conscience and the right of private judgment ', whilst the United Presbyterian Church explicitly allowed ' liberty of opinion on such points in the Standards, not entering into the substance of the faith, as the interpretation of the " six days " in the Mosaic account of the creation '— an interesting watermark of the period.

The question is whether a more unambiguous relation to the Confession might not now be adopted. In 1887, prodding his own Church forward to the task of creed revision, Dr. Taylor Innes declared that ' the Free Church, distinguished in its earlier time for *élan* and initiative, has of late changed its character, and for years past has been lying like a log in the trough of the waves '. It may be that the new forces of thought and service stirred by the coming union of the Scottish

Churches will lead to some fresh Confession of Faith being formulated, to interpret the Gospel succinctly in terms of modern thought to the world. The demands of to-morrow in missions and the altered outlook in science and philosophy may force this upon Churches which are by their genius and traditions tenacious of the older creeds. Presbyterianism, it may be said, is older than Calvinism, although it has been identified with Calvinism since the sixteenth century. In almost every Presbyterian Church which has taken any part in leadership of thought and action, the traditional standards of scholastic Calvinism have been modified; the Churches have sat looser to these formulas, either relaxing the terms of subscription or disavowing this or that inference from certain articles in the light of fuller Christian experience. It may be the lot of the Presbyterian Churches to draw up in the near future a Confession of Faith which is more adequate than any of the past creeds to the requirements of our age. There are vital movements in some of the Churches, particularly among the younger members, which are inspired by the hope and desire of such a formulation of doctrine. Many members are content, no doubt, with the historic creeds of the early centuries, and satisfied to retain the Westminster Confession of Faith as a symbol, under some formula or declaration which preserves their intellectual conscience. But this conservative attitude, from however worthy reasons it may be adopted, fails to satisfy others. The likelihood is that the problem of creed revision will become insistent before long.

IV

Yet, whatever be the form which a new creed or a re-interpretation of the old creed may take, it will certainly conserve one or two essential elements in Calvinism, not necessarily in the Five Points of Calvinism (which arose in the sharp struggle with Arminianism), but in the more gracious, essential Calvinism which, stripped of scholastic formulas, sought religious interests that are fundamental. If and when the Presbyterian Churches undertake the task of changing or revising their seventeenth-century creed, it will not involve dropping, for example (i), the profound sense of God's glory and majesty. The transcendent Will of God requires to be reinterpreted as a Will of redeeming love, in terms of the revelation in Jesus Christ. But in any reinterpretation the deep sense of awe and indebtedness and obligation to God must be preserved. It is characteristic of our Presbyterian traditions that neither the activities nor the emotions of the soul are regarded as the basis of assurance. All rests upon God's will or glory. This may be readily misinterpreted as the arbitrary will of a Deity jealous of His honour, but originally it was not so. R. L. Stevenson once wrote an essay on ' The Foreigner at Home ', as he pleasantly called the Englishman, and in noting the differences of national temperament he observed that ' the whole of the two divergent systems is summed up, not merely speciously, in the two first questions of the rival catechisms, the English tritely inquiring, " What is your name ? ", the Scottish striking at the very roots of life with, " What is the chief end of man ? " and answering nobly, if obscurely, " To glorify God and to enjoy Him for ever ". I do not wish to make an idol of the Shorter Catechism ; but the fact of such a question being asked opens to us Scotch the great field of speculation ; and the fact that it is asked of all of us, from the peer to the ploughboy, binds us more nearly together.' Alas, it is no longer asked, for the Shorter Catechism has waned like the use of porridge from the northern land. Still, there the question and the answer lie. And it was Carlyle, like Stevenson no rigid Presbyterian, who confessed towards the end of his life, ' The older I grow, and I am now upon the brink of eternity, the more comes back to me the first sentence of the Catechism which I learned when a child, and the fuller and deeper its meaning becomes, " What is the chief end of man ? To glorify God and to enjoy Him for ever " .' The ethical discipline of life is here regarded as obedience to the will of God in every sphere. That is fundamental to Calvinism. Hence the supreme interest in religion is conceived to be, not the human soul in relation to its destiny, but the glory or the will of God, by which the destinies of mankind as a whole and as individuals are determined. This may be stated in an utterly repulsive and arid fashion, alike in credal statement and popular teaching. Nothing is more easy than to caricature it or to misstate it. Yet there is religious value in its protest against a facile emotionalism, which tends to make Christianity revolve around the feelings and fears of the human heart. ' Remember that faith is one thing and the feeling and notion of faith another ; God forbid that this were good reasoning, " No feeling, no faith " .' And that is from the *Letters* of Samuel Rutherford ! He appears, as we have seen, too emotional for many in our day. But here he is in line with the trend of true Calvinism in recalling Christians to the action of God which underlies and inspires all experience. This better Calvinism, which was never quite lost, even amid the ungracious, controversial forms which the system assumed in more than one of our older Presbyterian statements, taught men that their first concern was to put God first, to regard themselves as His creatures, and to interpret life through His will and order ; it sought to impress on them the truth that Christianity is not a state of our consciousness, nor an experience of God which by our aspirations we produce and enjoy, but a relationship between God and ourselves in which we depend utterly on Him. The chief end of religion, accordingly, is to satisfy our Lord, not to satisfy our own feelings or to gratify our desires for safety and comfort. In an age when so many are preoccupied with the psychological analysis of the soul, or with experimental religion, it is and it will continue to be increasingly needful for the Churches to maintain this witness to the objectivity of religion.

(ii) The truth of God's will as all-embracing runs out into many applications. It is the source, for example, of that conception of the Church and the ministry which we have seen to be a vital element of Presbyterianism. To the genuine Calvinist, it is not of the will of man that the Church came into existence, any more than that salvation becomes real ; the Church is in a true sense the direct creation of God. But this has been sufficiently seen already, I hope. A more timely and less obvious application of the same truth is to be noted in the realm of social service, where the summons to the Church is felt to-day in every country with increasing urgency. Here again it is essential to maintain the rights of Christianity as religion. For there are some who in all good faith seek to recommend Christianity as a good religion for men to use in the development of life. Politicians have often considered it from the point of view of practical efficiency, as a cohesive or a revolutionary force, to be patronized for their own purposes or to be harnessed to some preconceived scheme of State welfare. Others start with the criterion, ' What is the God whom I can use in fulfilling my existence and discharging my duties as a citizen ? '. And they may decide that the Christian God is upon the whole the most useful and effective. That is, the programme for betterment is formed, and then as much or as little of Christianity is called in as they think needful for their immediate purposes. Now Calvinism, if it means anything, means that we do not form ideas and plans about life and then summon God to help us to carry them out. In an energetic age like ours the deep obligations of the social gospel require to be so interpreted that Christianity is not valued for its fruits, without due heed to its roots. Calvinism, as the Presbyterian Churches have seen it (that is, in their hours of true vision), bore on the social reorganization of life. Its very insistence on the enforcement of sanctity was due to the belief that the will of God required to be acknowledged throughout all departments of human life ; indeed, education, the care of the sick and the poor, and the general responsibility of the community for the individual, were regarded as functions of the Church, working in co-operation with the State as powers ordained of God. The individual must feel responsible for the community or for the Church ; that

public spirit or conscience for Church government was
one side of Calvinistic ethics, for all their limitations.
But the other side was equally true, the responsibility
of the larger community for health of soul and mind and
body in each of its constituent members. ' For Calvin ',
as Troeltsch remarks,[1] ' Christian ethic prescribed not
the mere recognition and endurance of worldly authority,
but the formation and maintenance of a reigning
authority which should correspond to the Christian
end of life and to the Word of God.'   It is this combina-
tion of care for social welfare and of a paramount
sense of Christianity as inherently authoritative that
marks out the healthier Calvinism. Hence, while
Christianity may be and must be applied to the social
problem, there must be no word of simply adjusting its
religious principles to suit propaganda which has been
independently drawn up. Nowadays our Church in
some lands has less direct influence over such services
as education and poor relief and healing than once she
had.   Still here and elsewhere the duty of this concern
remains, even although it may fall more on individuals
than on the corporate Church. And it is vital to
ensure that the concern is fundamentally religious, even
while the will of God is interpreted afresh in terms of
brotherhood and good will, after the mind of Jesus
Christ.   As any Church maintains this, it is supported,
non tam fama sed sua vi ; its own weight, its acceptance
of religious as well as of social responsibilities, keeps it
steady and sends it forward.

Wherever Presbyterian Churches have been content
to make worship a kind of luxury and to neglect the

---

[1] In his essay on ' Calvin and Calvinism,' in *The Hibbert
Journal* (October 1909), p. 117.

moral issues of the country, by allowing, for example, the goodness and comfort of one class to depend upon conditions which unfairly handicap another in the community, wherever any such failures in social justice and humane consideration have occurred, it has been due to a forgetfulness of ideas and visions which are thus enshrined in the Calvinistic conviction of God's will as an all-embracing authority for the various spheres of common life. In a word, my argument is that our Presbyterian Churches do not require to go beyond the implicates of their inherited Calvinism in order to discover sound religious motives for the enterprise of the social gospel. For Calvinism at its truest has never been satisfied until it has made the Christian conscience a power in the public life of the country. Evangelical Christianity has still to realize this, here and there. Indeed, all Churches have, who believe in the holy catholic Church.

> What *is* a holy Church unless she awes
> The times down from their sins?

But Churches with Calvinism behind them ought of all Churches to be most free from the reproach levelled against organized forms of Christianity, that they become indifferent to humanity. Whatever be the case to-day, it is to be hoped that to-morrow the Churches will be more alive to the fact that their spiritual freedom, if it is to be more than a facile phrase, means freedom to commend the Gospel far and wide, to develop the social conscience, and to impress upon its members that arrogance and unbrotherliness and worldliness are really heresies in the eyes of Christ.

Such are some of the central issues which, in an

N

analysis of the Presbyterian tradition, I consider urgnet
in our contemporary situation.   They constitute a test,
but the test is at once an honour and an opportunity.
So conservative a Church leader as the late Principal
Rainy in Scotland—conservative, I mean, in theology—
once wrote these timely words in a pamphlet : ' We
cannot be let alone.   Questions rise for us whether we
will or no. . . . The Church is obliged to let drop the
mere habits of her history, which suffice no longer, and
to take up her responsibilities as standing on the ground
and dealing with the work and the destiny of the catholic
Church of God.   Just by questions that come when we
would fain be let alone, God teaches us how great and
arduous a thing it is to *be* that Church and to follow
out her calling and her work.'   If that was true in 1867,
it is more true than ever to-day in 1927.   To-morrow
it is unlikely to be less true.

*   *   *   *   *

In the postscript of a letter to the Rev. Mr. Cole,
written on July 12, 1778, Horace Walpole tells his
correspondent, ' I like Popery as well as you, and have
shown that I do.   I like it as I like chivalry and romance.
They all furnish one with ideas and visions which
Presbyterianism does not.'   Horace Walpole's religious
likes and dislikes are not specially important ; when a
man talks about Wesley's services as an opera, he is
passing judgment on himself, not upon the religion he
is patronizing.   But what Walpole felt about Presbyterianism may be still felt by some, and I hope that if
this book does anything it may do something to dispel
such an illusion.   I write these closing words on July 12,
1927.   During the last century and a half Presby-

terianism has changed, as every living thing is bound to change. It had ideas and visions even when Walpole lived, though they were hidden from his modish eyes. It still has. And they are not survivals of the past, honoured merely for their antiquity, but, as I trust the readers of this book may grant, living ideas and visions such as a truly Christian and catholic Church cannot fail to enjoy and to impart, when its message and mission continue to be inspired by the spirit of the apostle's words, ' I speak of Christ and of the Church '.

INDEX

PRINTED IN GREAT BRITAIN
BY UNWIN BROTHERS, LIMITED
LONDON AND WOKING